Linux for Beginners

WHY YOU'RE NOT USING LINUX YET AND HOW TO OVERCOME COMMAND LINE FEAR

Nathan Clark

Absolute Life Publishing

WYOMING - USA

Nathan Clark
support@nathanclarkcoding.com

Ordering Information:
Quantity sales. Special discounts are available on quantity purchases by corporations, associations, and others. For details, contact the "Special Sales Department" at the address above.

Linux for Beginners / Nathan Clark. —2nd ed.
ISBN 979-8581926437

Complementary Books

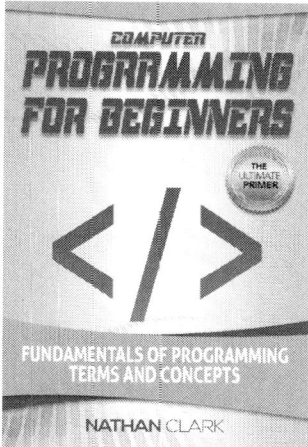

Programming for Beginners

Fundamentals of Programming
Terms and Concepts

Contents

About This Book

Have you tried to install Linux in the past only to get stuck with a broken system, eventually giving up and resorting back to your old Windows or macOS? Or are you overwhelmed by which distribution to choose, using a terminal for the first time, or simply being able to perform the tasks you normally would on your old system?

It may take you weeks to adjust to the Linux filesystem, right?
Wrong.

Linux is increasingly becoming more popular, with companies like Google, Facebook and IBM using Linux in one form or another. This is due to its superior privacy, reliability and security. Fortune Business estimates that the Linux market will increase by 402% in the next 7 years, making **now** the best time to get started with Linux. So, if the mythical Linux learning curve is holding you back, don't let it. We call it a myth, because with the right step-by-step guidance, that is exactly what it is - a myth.

Just because you're a beginner, doesn't mean it should be hard.

This book has been created to guide you through your very first steps in the Linux environment. If you are a complete novice or need a refresher in Linux, you've chosen the right book.

In the upcoming chapters we take a detailed look at the Linux diversity and history, and then continue with setting up a Linux system from scratch. Here we will guide you through the setup and configuration process step by step.

We will take a detailed look at the infamous command line by covering numerous essential terminal commands. We will also address specific topics such as choosing a distribution, adding a graphical user interface, package management, navigating the filesystem and directories, partitioning, software selection, and using the help system.

We also look at the administration and management tasks required to keep a Linux system running. It includes network security, user and group management, working with libraries, hardware and software management, interpreting log files, and other aspects every proficient Linux user should know.

For the examples in this book, we use the Debian Linux distribution as a reference point. However, the majority of the explanations apply to most distributions, especially Debian-based distributions such as Ubuntu, Mint, Pop! and Kali. Debian is merely what we use and prefer due to its outstanding stability. You are more than welcome to use a different Linux distribution.

By the end of this book you will have set up and configured Linux from start to finish, and be able to use Linux at a proficient level.

## CHAPTER ONE

What is Linux?

L inux is the name for the kernel of an operating system that is based on the UNIX principles. The name is derived from the first name of its Finnish inventor, Linus Torvalds, and follows the methodology used by other UNIX-based systems (the last letter is an x). Today, Linux is developed and maintained by thousands of people around the world.

The kernel of an operating system is its heart. It is required for communication between the hardware of your computer and you, the user. An operating system is a collection of different software components: a kernel, various tools, and the accompanying libraries. It is a software that extends the basic operating system of your computer, known as the BIOS.

From UNIX to Linux

The history of Linux can be traced back to the 1990s. To understand the story behind Linux, we also have to look back briefly at the early days of computing after the 2nd World War. At that time computing machines filled entire buildings and the transformation from mechanical to electronic components, like microprocessors and the usage of multi-layer circuits, was underway. Moreover, in the 1960s and 1970s hardware and software components were quite expensive and not standardized. Various vendor-specific platforms existed and each of them had their own interface, protocols to transfer and exchange data, as well as operating system. The communication between these single computing devices required specific knowledge and an understanding of its protocols. The development of UNIX was an aim to circumvent these obstacles and to simplify the usage of computing devices on a larger scale.

UNIX

At the beginning of 1965, the development of the Multiplexed Information and Computing Service (Multics) started. Multics was the result of a collaboration between the Massachusetts Institute of Technology (MIT), General Electric (GE) and Bell Labs/AT&T. Led by the developers Ken Thompson and Dennis Ritchie, the main product they developed was Unics. Later on it was renamed to UNIX. The UNIX operating system was mainly in use at the University of California in Berkeley.

UNIX Variants

The concept of UNIX became licensed to several companies that developed and maintained their own variant of UNIX. This included Solaris/SUN OS (SUN Microsystems nowadays owned by Oracle), AIX (IBM), Scenix (Siemens), SCO UNIX, Xenix (Microsoft), as well as HP-UX (Hewlett-Packard), NeXTSTEP, Mac OS (Apple), and Android (Google).

Open-source implementations comprised of the Berkeley System Distribution (BSD) with its variants: NetBSD, OpenBSD, and FreeBSD. Today, Linux is the most popular free software among open source developers. There is also strong commercial support for the systems mentioned above.

The UNIX Philosophy

UNIX is designed with several strict principles in mind. These principles cover portability, multi-tasking, and multi-user orientation in combination with a time-sharing approach. Furthermore, it is based on network connectivity following the TCP/IP scheme.

The original development was done in the C programming language that resulted in independence from a hardware platform. Delivered with a selection of development tools and libraries, it allows you to easily extend it to your specific needs. It is simple but has a powerful ability to automate tasks that supports complex but maintainable scripts.

Similar to a toolbox, UNIX consists of a variety of tools. Each of them having a specific purpose and being designed exactly for that task. The idea is to use one tool per task. To achieve more complex goals, you would combine several tools into a chain. The following example combines the two commands **ls** and **wc** employing a pipe to be able to count the number of Python files in the current directory.

```
$ ls *.py | wc -l
6
$
```

We will explain these commands and their usage in more detail later on in the guide.

A Brief History of Linux

Similar to UNIX, the Linux operating system has different roots and is based on the work of quite a few masterminds. Among others, this includes Richard M. Stallman, Andrew S. Tanenbaum, and Linus Torvalds.

Richard M. Stallman, a hacker and developer at MIT, is the first president of the Free Software Foundation (FSF), and the father of the GNU project. GNU abbreviates the slogan GNU is Not UNIX. The goal of the project was to develop a free UNIX operating system. Until the beginning of the 1990s, a collection of tools was available but the kernel was still missing. The entire software was published under the GNU Public License (GPL) around 1983.

The next step for Linux came from Andrew S. Tanenbaum. At that time he was a professor at the University of Amsterdam. For his students he developed Minix, an operating system for educational purposes to demonstrate and understand the UNIX principles. As he pointed out, Minix was not intended to be used in practice.

Linus Torvalds, a Finish student at the University of Helsinki, was a user of Minix and quite unhappy with its boundaries. In 1990 he began to develop a new operating system based on the ideas of Minix, the UNIX principles, and the POSIX standard. His motivation was to have his own system that was understandable and maximized to the boundaries of the hardware. He also wanted to have fun and had no commercial intent in mind. The entire story behind Linux is described in his autobiographical book titled *Just for Fun*. Today, Linus Torvalds oversees the development of the Linux kernel.

To make Linux attractive to the outside world it needed a nice logo. Based on a competition for mascots, a large number of proposals were handed in. Larry Ewing sent in his idea for a penguin as seen on the cover of this book, and his proposal won. Designed with a cheeky smile and a well-fed body, this penguin named Tux represents the image of a happy and satisfied user.

Linux Range of Use

Originally designed for Intel-based systems, Linux runs on a variety of platforms today. Among others, this includes the ARM architectures (named arm and arm64), Motorola / Freescale's 68k architecture (m68k), Intel x86 (i386 and amd64), IBM s390 (s390), PowerPC (powerpc), and SPARC (sparc).

Right from the beginning, Linux focused on server systems. It is widely used as a web server, file server, mail and news server, internet gateway, wireless router, and firewall. Used as a computing unit, it helped to render video sequences and entire films such as Titanic, Shrek, and Toy Story. Furthermore, Linux is in use in automotive products, astronautics, military, logistics, and the engineering environment. Since 2006, Linux servers run all the world's stock exchanges. It also runs almost all internet search engines.

Over the last decade Linux also conquered the desktop. Due to its high flexibility and stability, it works as a reliable setup for text processing, graphic design, desktop publishing, calculations in spreadsheets, communication (email, chat, audio, and video) as well as user interfaces for your phone and television.

Linux Certifications

The widespread use of Linux has increased the demand for engineers and users who know exactly what they are doing. At this point a certification for Linux becomes advantageous. These certifications can be divided into programs that are general (not specific to a distribution) and focused (specific to a Linux distribution). The lists below give an overview of the primary certifications that currently exist.

Non-specific Certifications

- Linux Essentials
- LPIC-1: Linux Server Professional Certification

- LPIC-2: Linux Engineer
- Linux Foundation Certified System Administrator (LFCS)
- Linux Foundation Certified Engineer (LFCE)
- CompTIA A+
- CompTIA Network+

Distribution-specific Certifications

- RedHat Certified Engineer (RHCE)
- RedHat Certified System Architect (RHCSA)
- RedHat Certified Architect (RCA)
- SUSE Certified Administrator (SCA)
- SUSE Certified Engineer (SCE)
- SUSE Enterprise Architect (SEA)

## CHAPTER TWO

Software Licenses

A s with most products available on the market, software is also packaged with a corresponding license. A software license describes the usage of the software and allows or limits its use. For commercial software, changes and copies are allowed within rather strict boundaries only. As an example, the license restricts you to use it for 5 users in parallel and requires you to obtain another license block to add a 6th or 7th user. Common licenses are Shared Source from Microsoft and the Apple License.

For open-source software, licenses are much less restrictive. Changes and copies are explicitly allowed and are even desired in some cases to make improvements for a specific user and purpose. The goal is to keep the software available for everyone from now and into the future. This so-called *Copyleft* principle ensures that everyone has access to do adaptations if needed, and the restrictions on the use and redistribution of covered software are as minimal as possible. Common licenses that are in use for the single Linux components and its tools are the GNU Public License (GPL), BSD Licenses, and the Apache License.

The licenses for open-source software follow several freedom rules:

- To use the program for every purpose (right of unlimited use - freedom 0).
- To understand how the program works and how to change it according to your needs (right to read the source code of the program - freedom 1).
- To make copies of the software to help your neighbor (right of redistribution - freedom 2).
- To improve the software and to publish your changes so that all other users can also benefit from your improvements (freedom 3).

This ensures that the quality of available software constantly improves and everyone has access to these improvements. Using the GPL, the changes have to be published using the same license. Other open-source licenses like BSD do not have this strong requirement.

## CHAPTER THREE

Linux Distributions

There are a few terms that may confuse Linux beginners. The first one is its name, Linux vs GNU/Linux. As described earlier in Chapter 1, the term Linux refers to the Linux kernel only. In reality, many users refer to Linux as the operating system as a whole, including the kernel, libraries, and tools. The term Linux is also used in practice to include all the programs that run on Linux, or that are available for this operating system.

Furthermore, the description GNU/Linux needs some explanation. Linux distributions with this name prefix are fleshed out with GNU implementations of the system tools and programs. One such example is Debian GNU/Linux. As already pointed out in Chapter 1, the GNU project goes back to the initiative of Richard M. Stallman and his dream to develop a free UNIX system.

Based on his experiences at MIT and the collaboration with other colleagues, he chose to use free software that was already available to rewrite the tools he needed. This included the TeX typesetting system as well as the X11 window system.

He published the rewritten tools under the GPL license whenever possible to make his work available freely to everyone interested in it.

What is a Linux Distribution?

A Linux distribution is a collection of software packages that fit together. A distribution is maintained by a team of software developers, and each member of the team focuses on a different package of the distribution. Together as a team, they ensure that the single software packages are up-to-date and do not conflict with other packages of the same release.

As of 2020 for Debian GNU/Linux 10, the official repositories contain more than 59,000 different packages. A repository is a directory of packages with a specific purpose. Debian GNU/Linux sorts its packages according to the development state. The official repository is named *stable* and reflects the current release of stable packages. The other repositories are named *testing* and *unstable*, and work in the same way but do not count as official packages.

Typically, a Linux distribution comprises of packages for a Linux kernel, a boot loader, GNU tools and libraries, a graphical desktop environment with a windows environment, as well as additional software like a web browser, an email client, databases, and documentation. The software is provided in two ways, as the source code and as the compiled binary packages. This allows you to understand how the software is designed, to study it, and to adjust it according to your personal needs. This step is described as *freedom 1* on the list shown in Chapter 2.

Depending on the focus of the Linux distribution, it also contains packages for a specific purpose like network or forensic tools, scientific software for educational purposes, and multimedia applications. More details are given next.

Choosing a Linux Distribution

According to Distrowatch, more than 600 different Linux distributions exist. One of the major questions is: which Linux distribution to use? Based on our experience, we have the following recommendations:

For beginners	Ubuntu, Xubuntu, openSUSE, Linux Mint.
For advanced users	Debian, Red Hat Enterprise Linux (RHEL), Fedora, CentOS.
For developers	Arch Linux, Gentoo, Slackware.

For the examples in this book, we use Debian GNU/Linux. Even though this distribution is recommended for advanced users it is still very beginner-friendly, which we will demonstrate in this guide. But the most important reason for this selection is its stability and the trust we have in this distribution that was built up during the last 20 years of permanent use in our servers and desktop systems. Other Linux distributions fluctuate too much for our comfort. The biggest mistake we see beginners make, is choosing to install an unstable distribution at the start, which in many cases can ruin your entire Linux experience and put you off Linux completely.

You are more than welcome to choose a different Linux distribution. Just ensure it is one that doesn't have known stability issues. The majority of this book applies to most distributions. But if you are a complete novice, we highly recommend sticking to Debian at least for the duration of this guide, as we will go step by step through its setup and configuration. In general, choosing a distribution can depend on several criteria:

- The intended audience: end-user, network engineer, system administrator, developer.
- Its availability: free or commercial use.
- Its purpose: desktop, server, Wi-Fi network appliance.
- The package format: .deb, .rpm, .tar.gz.
- The frequency of available updates: every Linux distribution follows its own update cycle.
- The provided support: support can be free (community-based) or with costs (based on a support contract).

When selecting a distribution, we recommend one that is stable, that is updated regularly, and fits into the purpose you need the computer for. Coming up next, you will find a short description of each of the major Linux distributions.

⊚debian

Established in 1993, Debian GNU/Linux (Debian for short) is an entirely free and community-based operating system that follows the GNU principles. More than 1,000 developers continuously work on it of their own free will. There are no corporations behind the development of Debian, which means there are no business interests involved.

One design goal is to have a stable and reliable operating system for computers that are actively delivering services. It is targeted to users who know what they want, and the Debian developers maintain and use their own software. The packages are made available in .deb format and are divided into categories according to the following licenses:

- Main: free software.
- Contrib: free software dependent on non-free software.
- Non-free: packages that have a non-free license.

Debian works well on both servers and desktop systems. A range of architectures are supported like ARM EABI (arm), IA-64 (Itanium), MIPS, MIPSel, powerpc, s390 (32 and 64 bit), as well as sparc, i386 (32 bit) and amd64 (64 bit). The code name of each release is based on the name of a character from the film *Toy Story*, such as *Stretch* for Debian GNU/Linux 9 and *Buster* for Debian GNU/Linux 10.

ubuntu

Ubuntu is a free Linux distribution that is financed by the company Canonical Ltd. It is based on Debian but focuses on beginners instead. That's why it contains only one tool per task. The Ubuntu team is known to incorporate brand new elements that lack stability. This is one of the biggest complaints we receive when talking to newcomers. For this reason, we do not recommend Ubuntu to beginners. Popularity does not equal usability. Our number one recommendation is Debian, with Mint a good second choice.

The packages are made available in .deb format and are divided into categories according to their support from Canonical:

- Main: free software, supported by Canonical.
- Restricted: non-free software, supported by Canonical.
- Universe: free software, unsupported.
- Multiverse: non-free software, unsupported.

Ubuntu is available in three official editions: Ubuntu Desktop, Ubuntu Server, and Ubuntu Core (for the Internet of Things). A range of architectures is supported such as i386, IA-32, amd64, ARMhf (ARMv7 VFPv3-D16), ARM64, powerpc (64 bit), and s390x. Initially published in 2004, there are two releases per year: one in April and another in October. The release is reflected by the version number: 18.04 refers to the April release of the year 2018. The code name of a release is based on an adjective and an animal, such as Utopic Unicorn for Ubuntu 14.10.

Linux Mint aims to offer a more familiar desktop experience that Windows users will appreciate, along with having decent hardware and multimedia support out of the box. The Cinnamon Desktop version of Mint is a fan favorite for its close resemblance to a Windows environment, even supporting similar keyboard shortcuts. Due to its overall reliability, this a distribution we can comfortably recommend.

Mint is a non-commercial distribution that is based on Ubuntu and follows the same release scheme. The initial publication dates back to the year 2006. As of 2014, there have been two releases per year following the release from Ubuntu by one month. The code name for the release is a female name that ends with an *a*, such as Felicia for version 6. Linux Mint supports the two architectures IA-32 and amd64.

Red Hat Enterprise Linux (RHEL) is a commercial Linux distribution. It is based on the combination of Red Hat Linux (available between 1995 and 2004) plus Fedora 19 and 20. Its original release dates back to the year 2000. Its focus on business customers includes long-term support, training, and a certification program (see Chapter 1). Red Hat's community project is called Fedora (see the following page).

The packages are made available in .rpm format (Red Hat Package Manager). RHEL supports the architectures arm (64 bit), i386, amd64, powerpc, as well as s390 and zSeries. The distribution targets both servers and desktops. The code name for the release appears to be random, as it does not follow a similar scheme as used for Debian or Ubuntu.

Fedora is a community Linux distribution aimed mainly at desktop users. It is based on Red Hat Enterprise Linux (RHEL) and sponsored by Red Hat. It was launched in 2003 at the time the support for Red Hat Linux ended. As of 2020, it is available in the following versions:

- Workstation: for pc.
- Server: for servers.
- IoT: for IoT ecosystems.

Fedora supports the architectures amd64, armhf, powerpc, MIPS, s390, and RISC-V. The distribution has a rather short lifecycle where a new release follows roughly every 6 months. The code name for a release does not follow a fixed naming scheme but mostly consists of city names.

CentOS abbreviates from the name Community Enterprise Operating System. As with Fedora it is based on Red Hat Enterprise Linux and is compatible in terms of the binary packages. This allows the use of software on CentOS that is initially offered and developed with RHEL in mind. In contrast to Fedora, it focuses on enterprise use for both desktops and servers, with long-term support. The initial release of CentOS goes back to May 2004. CentOS is available for the architectures i386 and amd64. Other architectures are not supported. The software packages come from three different repositories:

- Base: regular, stable packages.
- Updates: security, bug fix, or enhancement updates.
- Addons: packages required for building the larger packages that make up the main CentOS distribution, but are not provided upstream.

The Linux distribution openSUSE has its roots in the distributions SUSE Linux and the commercial SUSE Linux Professional that saw its first release in 1994. The name SUSE is an abbreviation for the original German owner Gesellschaft für Software- und Systementwicklung GmbH.

OpenSUSE is based on the structures of Red Hat Linux and Slackware, and uses .rpm as a software archive format. It is available for the architectures i586, x86-64, and ARM. The openSUSE project aims to release a new version every eight months. As with Fedora, the code names for a release do not follow a fixed naming scheme.

Arch Linux is a free Linux distribution that saw its first release in 2002. It follows the principle of a rolling release, which results in monthly updates of the distribution. Currently, the core team consists of about 25 developers and is supported by many other developers, called *trusted users*. Arch Linux uses Pacman as a package management system. The single packages are held in four software repositories:

- Core: packages for the basic system.
- Extra: additional packages like desktop environments and databases.
- Community: packages maintained by trusted users.
- Multilib: packages used on several architectures.

Arch Linux supports the amd64 architecture. The early releases up to 2007 had code names that do not follow a specific scheme, with recent releases following a standard numbering format.

As with Arch Linux, Gentoo follows the principle of a rolling release. New installation images are available weekly, with the first release available in 2002. Gentoo is special due to being a source code-based distribution. Before installing the software, it has to be compiled first. Supported architectures are alpha, amd64, arm, hppa, IA-64, m68k, MIPS, powerpc, s390, sh, and sparc.

Slackware is the oldest active Linux distribution. The first release dates back to 1992. Regular releases are available without a fixed interval. It targets professional users and gives them as much freedom as possible. Slackware uses compressed tar.gz archives as a package format and supports the four architectures i486, alpha, sparc, and arm. The distribution was also ported to architecture s390.

## CHAPTER FOUR

Setting up a Linux System

A s mentioned in the previous chapter, we will be using Debian for our demonstrations. To recap, Debian is a distribution that provides great stability and scales up exceptionally well once your skills and knowledge progress past the beginner stages. In this chapter we will install and configure Debian, showing you every single step along the way.

Types of Installations

Debian offers a variety of methods for a proper setup. This includes a graphical and a text-based installation; we will use the former. For installation media the Debian developers offer three variants:

- A CD or DVD for 32-bit and 64-bit.
- A network image for 32-bit and 64-bit (a so-called Net-inst-ISO).
- A mini-CD for 32-bit or 64-bit.

We also have test media available. These include live images for 32-bit and 64-bit, and allow you to try Debian before installing it on your computer. During the time of writing this guide, version 10 is the current stable release of Debian. The setup described here is based on this release and the amd64 architecture.

After downloading the network image from the webpage www.debian.org/distrib no further static images are required. Instead, it depends on your internet connection to retrieve the packages to be installed and keep your operating system up-to-date.

The entire process will take you about an hour and it allows you to have a lean software selection based on your specific needs. Software packages that you do not use will not be available on your system. They can however be added whenever you feel the need.

The target system of our installation is an XFCE-based desktop system for a single user with a web browser and a music player. For the web browser we use Mozilla Firefox and for the music player, VLC. Both programs are a permanent component of the Linux distribution. The environment we use for demonstration purposes is a virtual machine based on VirtualBox with 4 GB of RAM and 8 GB of disc space.

Installing Linux Step-by-Step

Boot Menu

To begin with the installation of Debian, first boot the computer (in our case the VirtualBox image) from the ISO image you have downloaded. If you are also using a virtual machine, see your virtual machine vendor website for help on how to enable the ISO image. Next, wait for the boot menu to appear on the screen. The image on the adjacent page shows you the different options that are offered. Using the cursor keys, you can navigate the boot menu and the Enter key selects an entry.

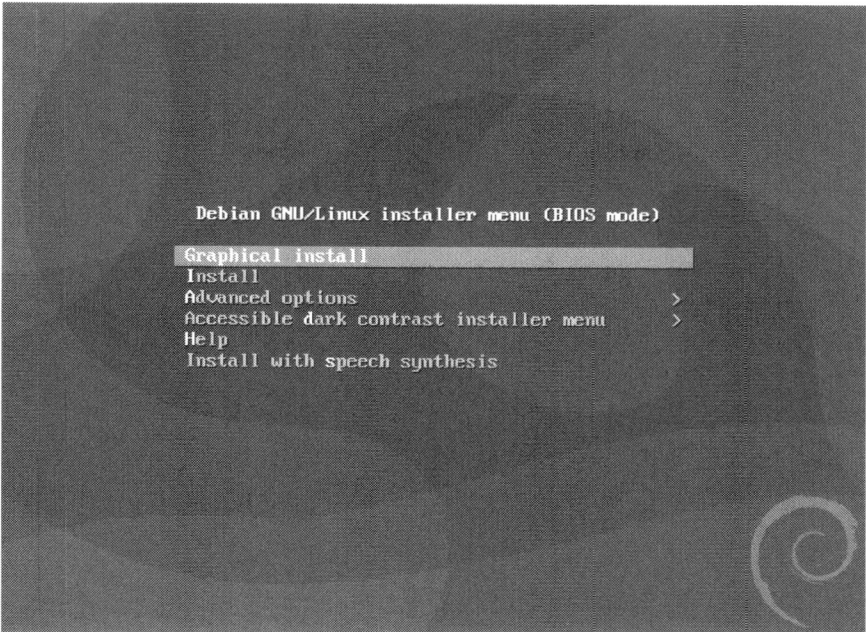

```
    Debian GNU/Linux installer menu (BIOS mode)

    Graphical install
    Install
    Advanced options                              >
    Accessible dark contrast installer menu       >
    Help
    Install with speech synthesis
```

The different options are:

Graphical install	Start the installation process using a graphical installer.
Install	Starting the installation process using a text-based installer.
Advanced options	Select further options like Expert mode, Automated install, or Rescue mode.
Dark contrast	Switch to a black-and-white theme with higher contrast.
Help	Get further help.
Speech synthesis	Starting the installation process with speech support.

From the main boot menu choose the entry *Graphical install*, and press the Enter key to proceed.

Language Selection

Next, choose the language you prefer to be used during the entire installation process. The dialogs and messages are translated accordingly. This selection does not irrevocably determine the language your Linux system will have, you can always choose a different language later.

The image below shows the dialog box. English is already pre-selected, and so you just have to click the Continue button on the lower-right corner of the dialog box to proceed.

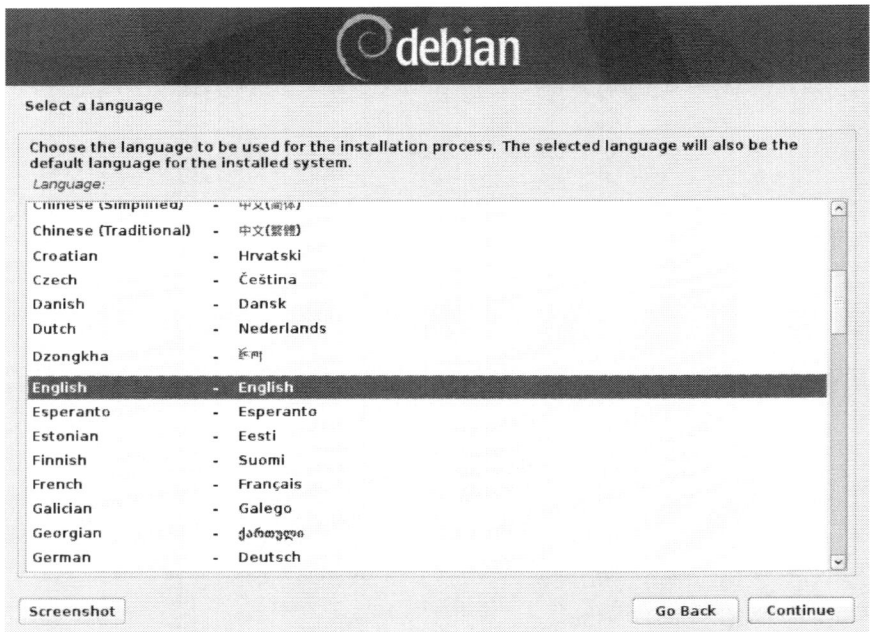

Location Selection

Third, make a selection regarding your location (see image below). Based on your language setting made before, the countries are listed in which the chosen language is mainly spoken. This also influences the locale settings like the time zone your computer is in. To have a different setting choose the entry titled *other* from the end of the list and go on from there. When you are done, click the Continue button to proceed with step four.

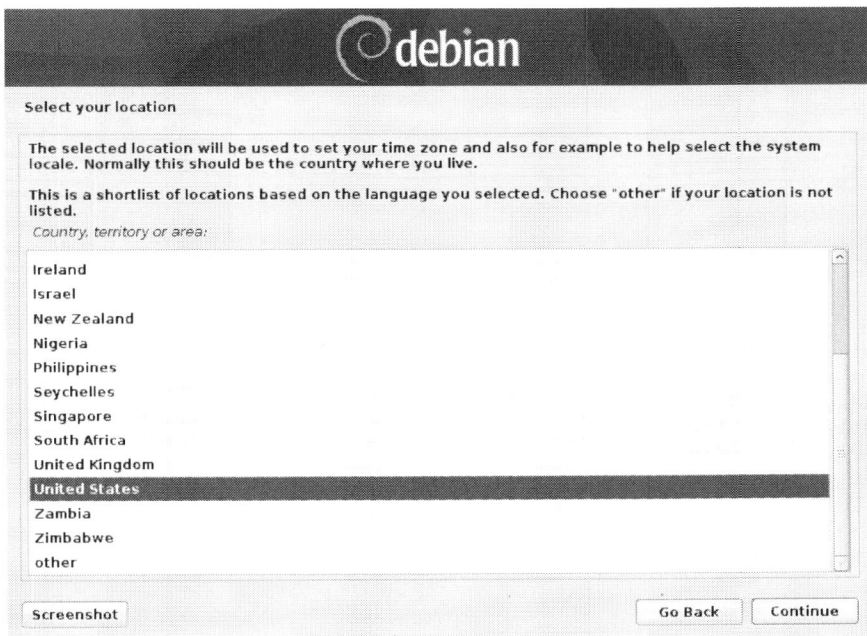

Keyboard Selection

Fourth, choose your keyboard layout from the list (see image on the following page). For the United States, the preselection is American English. If you use a different keyboard layout select the correct one from the list. If done click the Continue button to proceed with step five.

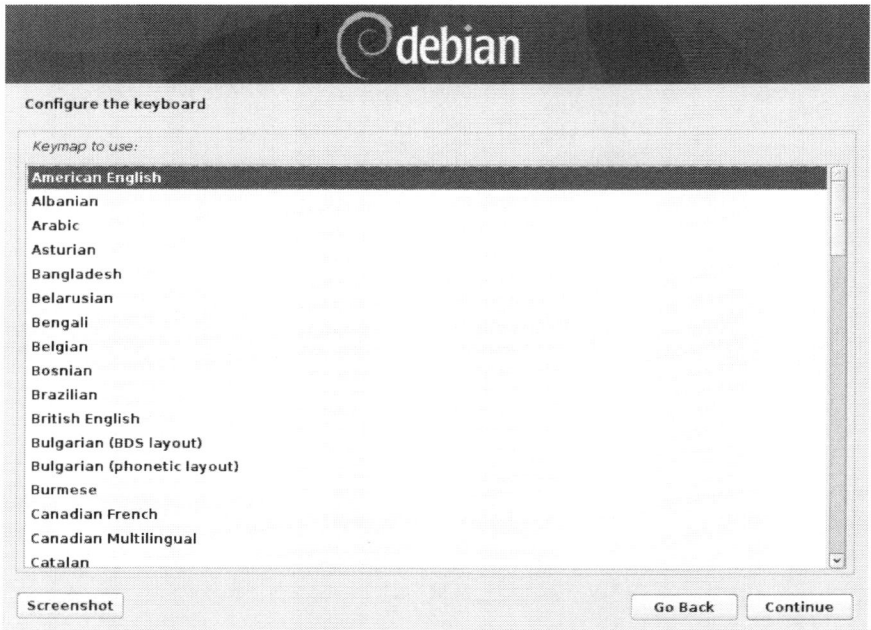

Network Setup

Step five includes loading the installer components from the ISO image, and the detection of the network hardware to load the correct network driver. Then, the installer tries to connect to the internet to retrieve an IP address via DHCP from your local network server.

When done, you can set up the hostname of your computer (see adjacent image). Choose a unique name for your machine that consists of a single name and does not exist yet in your local network segment. It is common to use names of fruits, places, musical instruments, composers, and characters from movies.

In this case, we choose the name *debian106* that simply represents the Linux distribution and its version number.

When you are done, click the Continue button to proceed with step six to add a domain name like *yourcompany.com*. In this case, it is not needed. That's why we leave the entry field empty. Click the Continue button on the lower-right corner to proceed with the installation.

Users and Roles

Our Linux system needs at least two users to be operated properly. One is an administrative user that has a fixed name *Root* and the other is a regular user that we just give the name of *User* in this case.

In the next two steps, you set the password for the root user and both the full name and account name for the regular user. For simplicity, we use *Debian User* as the full name and *User* as the account name. For both users, choose a password that is dissimilar and that you can remember. You will need these passwords later to log onto your computer.

Time Zone

Setting the correct time zone is of significant importance for communication with other services, especially in a network. Choose the value from the list as seen in the image on the next page. The entries in the list are based on the location you have selected before. When done, click the Continue button to define the storage media and the accompanying partitions.

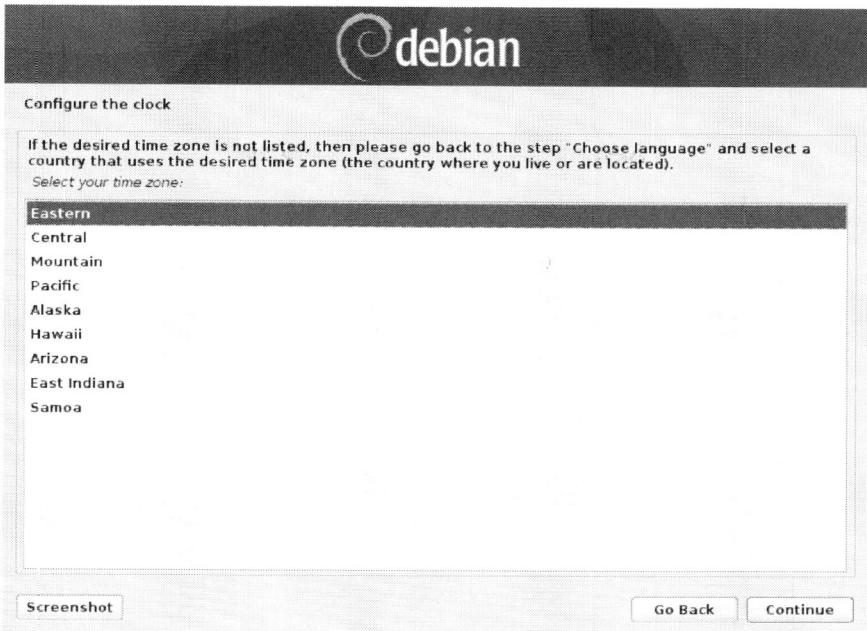

debian

Configure the clock

If the desired time zone is not listed, then please go back to the step "Choose language" and select a country that uses the desired time zone (the country where you live or are located).

Select your time zone:

Eastern
Central
Mountain
Pacific
Alaska
Hawaii
Arizona
East Indiana
Samoa

Screenshot   Go Back   Continue

Storage Media and Partitioning

A Linux system can be distributed across several different storage media like hard disks and flash drives. Over and above, storage media can be separated into multiple disk partitions. To do so, the setup program has the following methods available:

Guided - use entire disk

Follow the steps as provided and use the entire disk space for the Linux installation. This creates partitions with fixed sizes.

Guided - use entire disk and set up LVM

Follow the steps as provided and use the entire disk space for the Linux installation. This option makes use of Logical Volume Management (LVM) to create partitions with sizes that can be changed later on.

Guided - use entire disk and set up encrypted LVM

Follow the steps as provided and use the entire disk space for the Linux installation. This option makes use of Logical Volume Management (LVM) to create encrypted partitions with sizes that can be changed later on.

Manual

Create partitions individually. This is the expert mode and requires deeper knowledge about partitions and filesystem parameters.

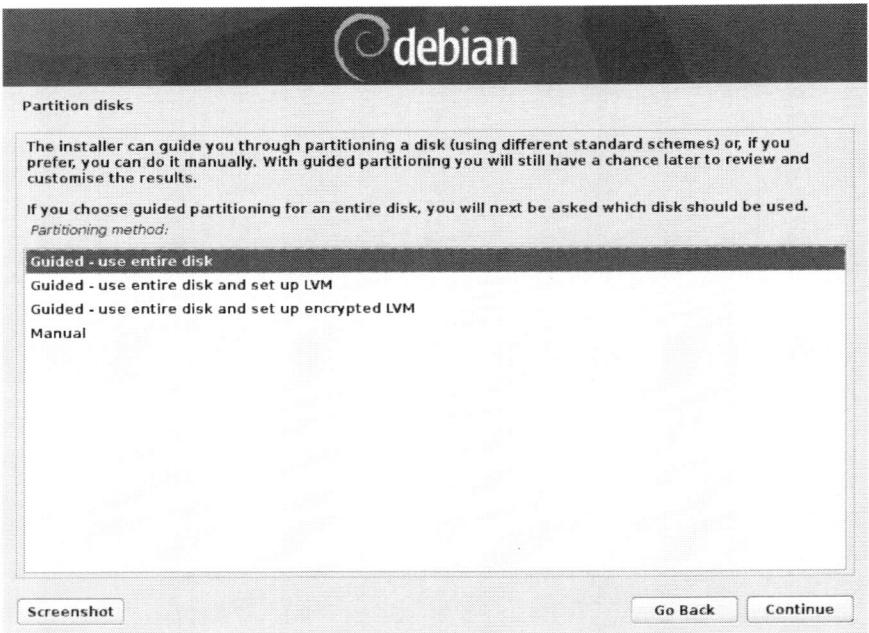

From the list choose the entry *Guided - use entire disk*. The values for partition sizes are chosen according to experience, implemented as an algorithm.

A manual calculation is not required. Click the Continue button on the lower-right corner to proceed with the installation. Next, select the disk to partition. In our case, we have only one disk available (see image below). Later on in this guide, the disk will be referred to as /dev/sda for the first SCSI disk.

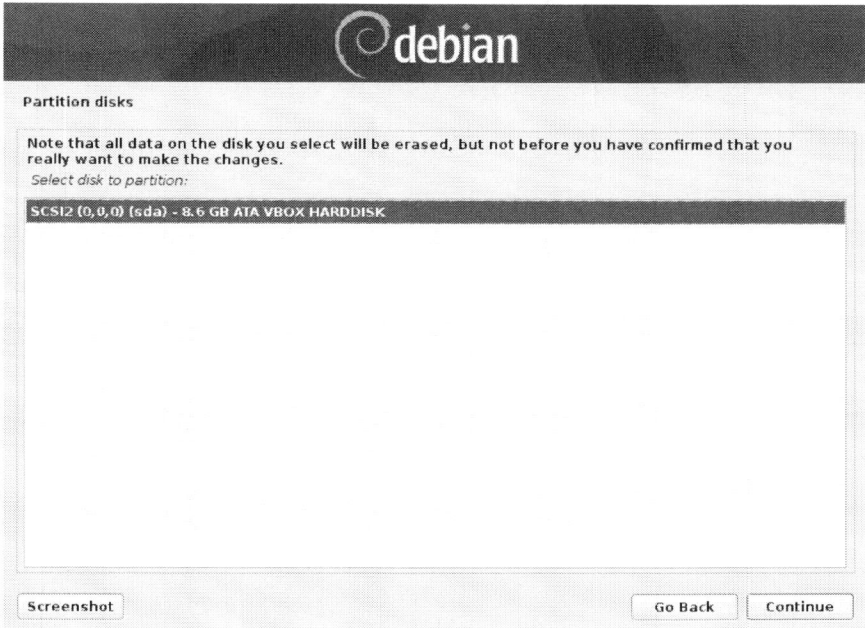

A disk partition refers to a piece of the storage media that is organized separately and is intended to contain a branch of the Linux filesystem tree. There is no universal way to do this separation correctly. This guide shows a simple but safe solution that works for a basic system. The menu in the dialog box offers the following options:

All files in one partition

Use a single partition to keep programs and user data.

Separate /home partition

Store programs and user data in separate partitions.

Separate /home, /var, and /tmp partitions

Keep user data, variable data and temporary data in separate partitions (available on some distributions).

As shown in the image below, choose the second entry *Separate /home partitions*. Click the Continue button to proceed with the installation.

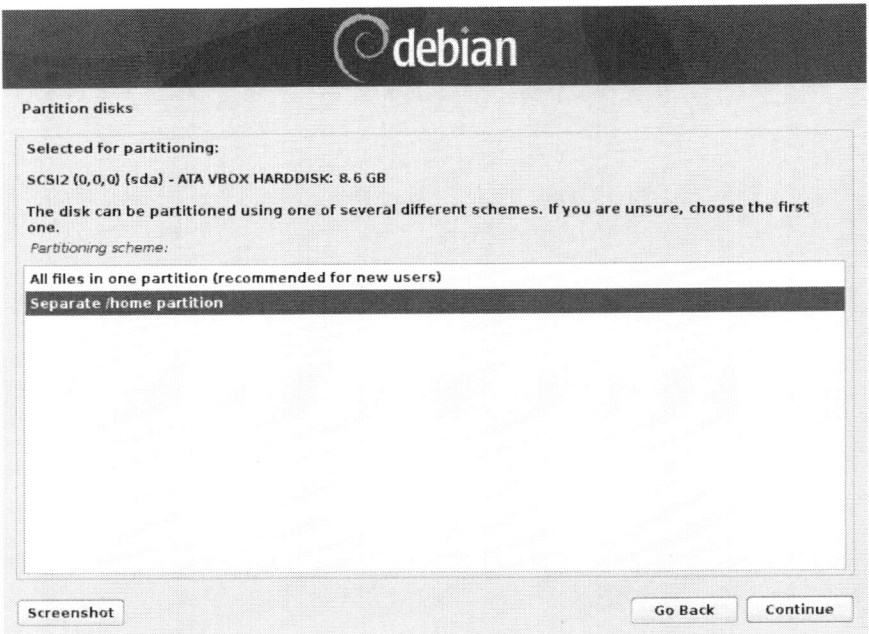

The next step is to confirm the partition scheme. This is calculated automatically based on experience and contains these partitions:

sda1 The first partition of the first SCSI disk is a primary partition with a size of 2.8 GB, formatted with the ext4 filesystem, and referred to as the root part of the filesystem tree (indicated with /).

sda5 The fifth partition of the first SCSI disk is a logical partition with a size of 2.1 GB, formatted as a swap filesystem.

sda6 The sixth partition of the first SCSI disk is a logical partition with a size of 3.6 GB, formatted with the ext4 filesystem and reserved to store user data, referred to as home directories (indicated with /home).

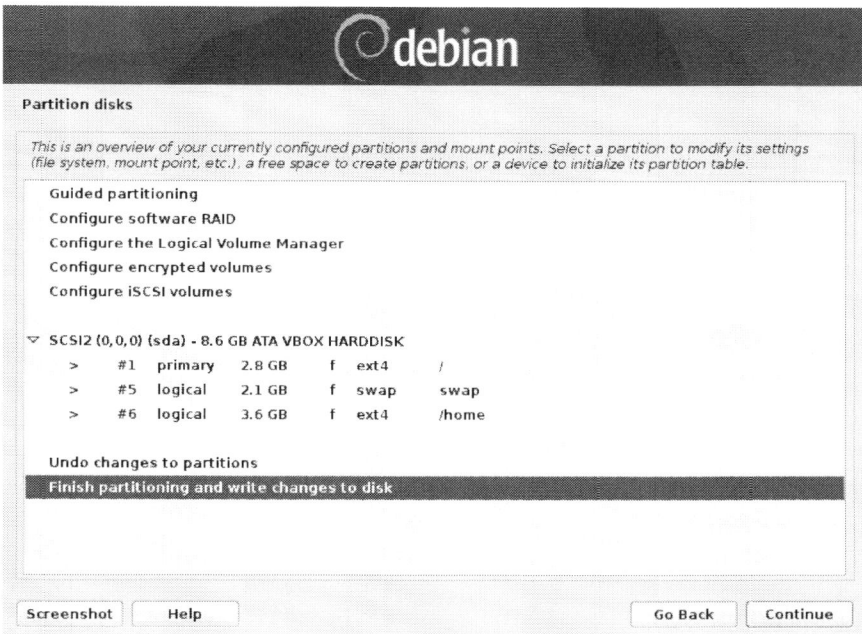

Due to historical reasons, a hard disk can contain four primary partitions only. The fourth one is called an *Extended Par-*

tition if divided into so-called logical partitions or logical drives. In our case the logical partitions /dev/sda5 and /dev/sda6 are stored on the primary partition /dev/sda4. The partitions /dev/sda2 and /dev/sda3 are not in use.

From the above list, choose the entry *Finish partitioning and write changes to disk*. Click the Continue button on the lower-right corner to proceed and to confirm the partition scheme (see image). Choose *yes* from the list and click the Continue button to partition the disk. Note that all the data on the select-ed storage device will be lost and the disk will be empty.

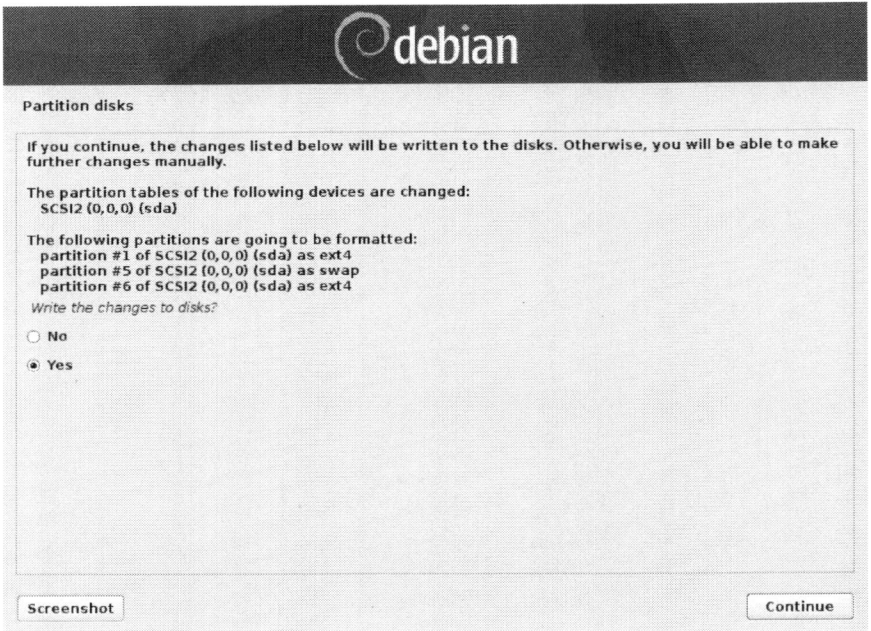

Having divided the storage media into single partitions, the partitions will be formatted with the filesystem as defined be-fore. In our case, the partitions /dev/sda1 and /dev/sda6 will get an ext4 filesystem, and the partition /dev/sda5 will get a swap filesystem. As soon as this step is completed, the base system of Debian will be installed next.

Package Management

The ISO image contains the installer and several packages to set up the Linux base system, including the Linux kernel. Next, you need to decide whether to use additional installation media or not. In our case, we have only a single installation disk and can consequentially select *No* from the menu (see below). Then click the Continue button to proceed.

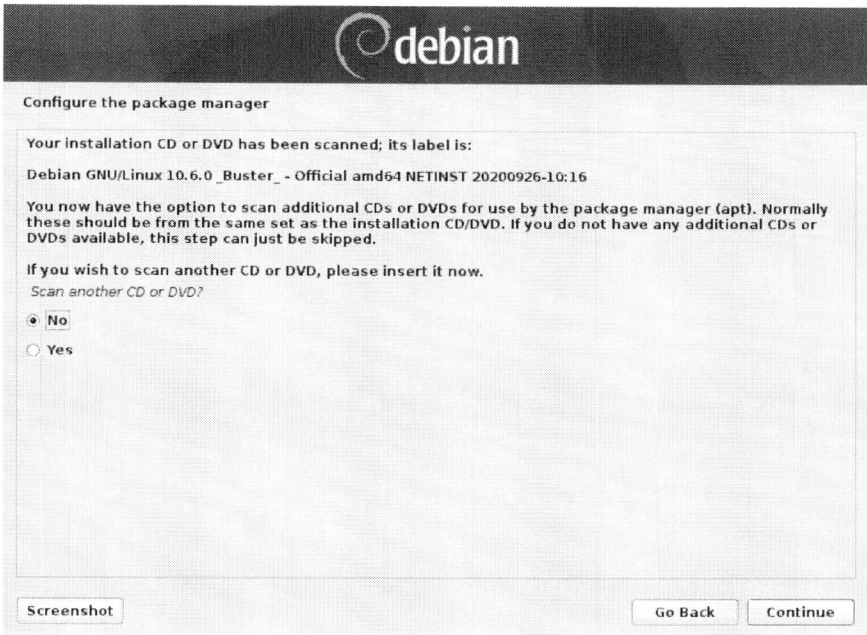

As pointed out earlier, the software for Debian is organized in packages. These packages are provided in multiple software repositories. The repositories are made available via package mirrors that are maintained by universities, private individuals, companies, and other organizations. These mirrors are located in different countries.

In the next step, you will have to decide from which country you would like to retrieve your Debian packages. It is recommended to choose a mirror that is geographically located near you to minimize the time that is needed to transport the data from the mirror to your computer via network. As an initial step, choose your desired country.

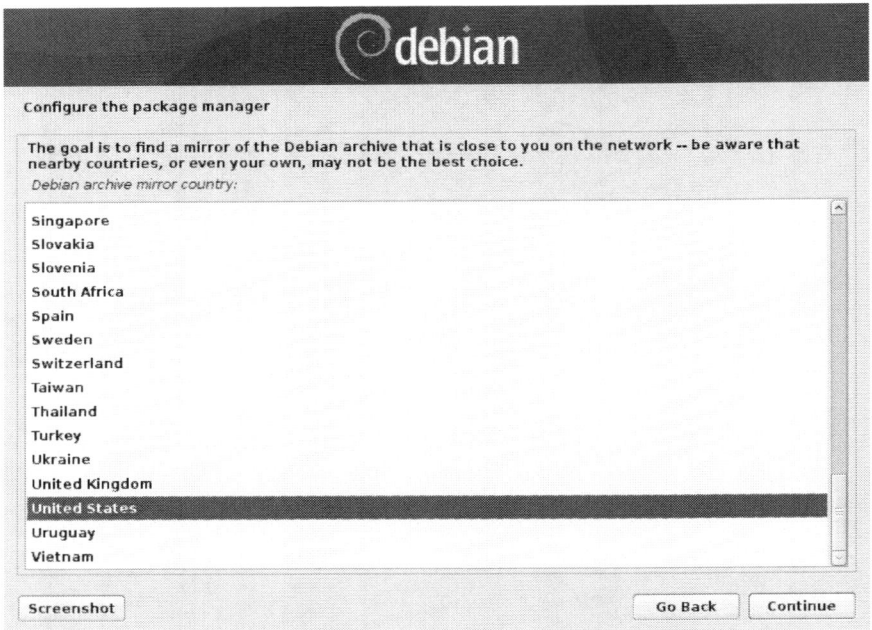

As a second step, choose a preferred mirror from the list (see adjacent page). The list contains universities, internet providers, government services, and other organizations.

debian

Configure the package manager

Please select a Debian archive mirror. You should use a mirror in your country or region if you do not know which mirror has the best internet connection to you.

Usually, deb.debian.org is a good choice.

Debian archive mirror:

ftp.us.debian.org
debian.csail.mit.edu
debian.osuosl.org
debian.cc.lehigh.edu
debian.gtisc.gatech.edu
mirror.cc.columbia.edu
deb.debian.org
debian-archive.trafficmanager.net
mirrors.lug.mtu.edu
mirror.us.oneandone.net
mirrors.bloomu.edu
mirrors.namecheap.com
mirrors.ocf.berkeley.edu
debian.mirror.constant.com

Screenshot   Go Back   Continue

debian

Configure the package manager

If you need to use a HTTP proxy to access the outside world, enter the proxy information here. Otherwise, leave this blank.

The proxy information should be given in the standard form of "http://[[user][:pass]@]host[:port]/".

HTTP proxy information (blank for none):

Screenshot   Go Back   Continue

In case your computer network includes a proxy server to communicate with the outside world, enter the appropriate information in this screen. In this case, we don't have that and leave the entry field empty. Click the Continue button to proceed.

As soon as the single parameters are set, the Debian installer connects to the previously selected package mirror and retrieves the package lists from there. A package list contains the available packages, including the name, size, and description. Depending on the quality and bandwidth of your network connection this step can take a while.

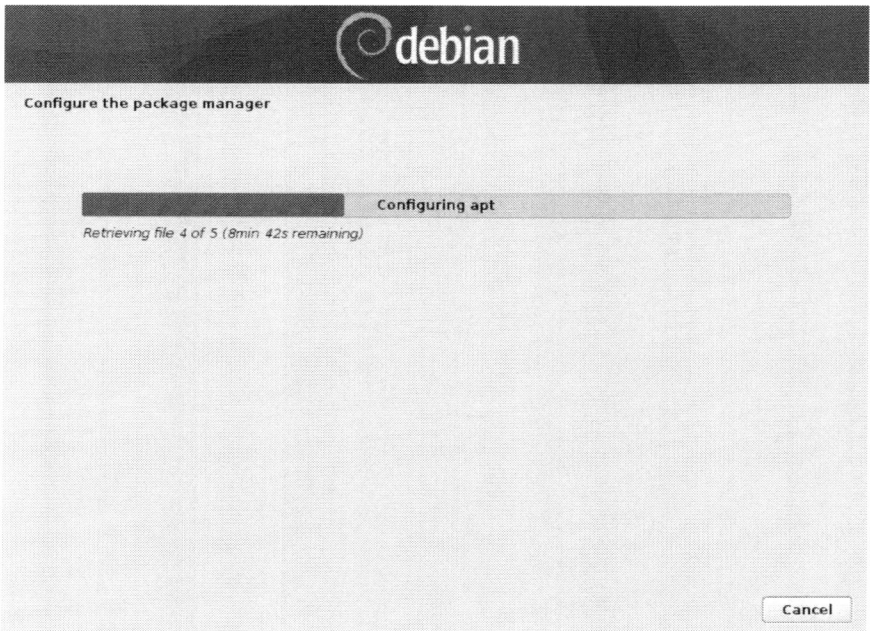

Next, you are asked to take part in *Popcon*, the Debian package popularity contest. This information is optional and is used only by the team of developers that is responsible for the Debian packages. Based on Popcon, they figure out which Debian packages are the ones that are installed most often. The information has a direct influence on the preparation of installation images and which packages to keep or to dismiss for the different architectures.

In our case, we do not participate in Popcon and leave the selection to *No*. Click Continue to proceed with the selection of software tasks (tasksel).

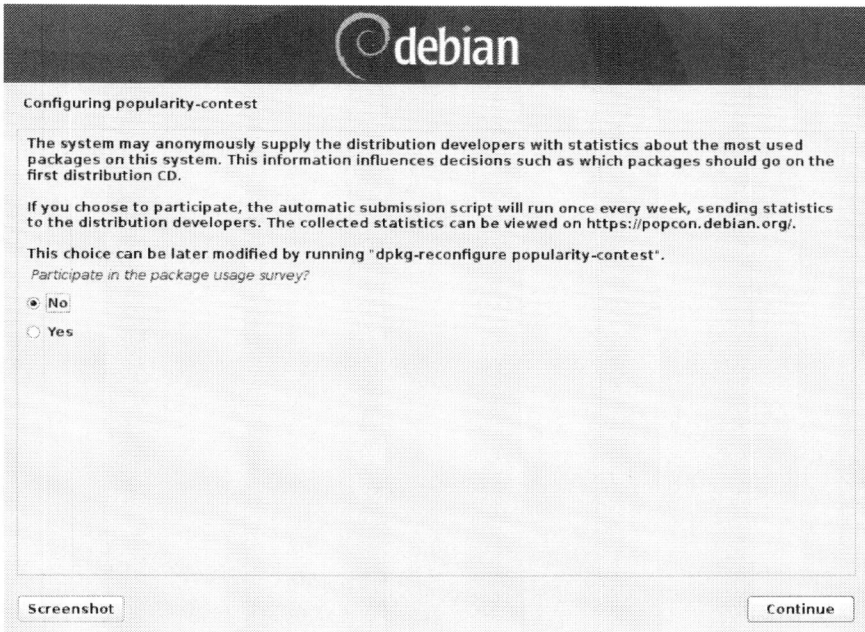

Software Selection

Debian offers carefully arranged selections of packages, so-called *tasks*. The idea behind them is to group packages for specific uses to simplify the installation. From the list in the dialog window (see following page) you can choose between different desktop environments, as well as a web server, a print server, an SSH server, and the standard system utilities. To have a lean installation, enable only the last two entries from the list. We will install the XFCE desktop environment later.

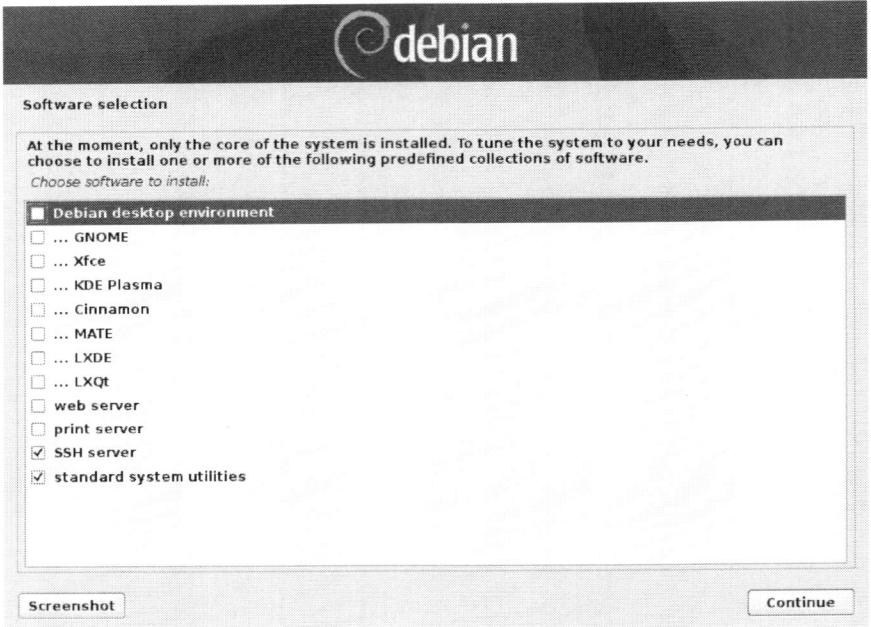

Having confirmed the software selection, the Debian installer retrieves the needed packages from the package mirror, unpacks, and then installs them. The progress bar shows the installation progress.

Setting up GRUB

To start our newly installed Debian system, we have to set the startup information as well. This process is called *booting* the system. The software component that handles this step is named Grand Unified Boot Loader (GRUB or GNU GRUB to be precise). Select *Yes* and click Continue to proceed.

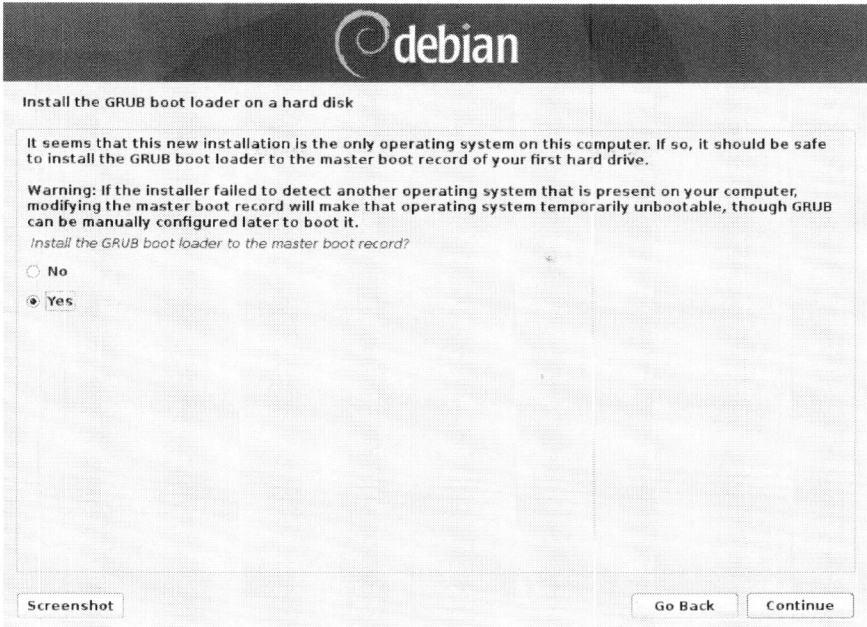

The Debian installer needs to know where to install GRUB. The menu in the previous image lists the storage media to be considered. In our case, we choose the second entry from the list (/dev/sda). Then, click Continue to proceed. Now that we are nearly finished with the basic installation, the only thing left to do is a single dialog box to read.

Finishing the Installation

The following dialog box informs you that the installation is complete. Then click Continue to reboot the newly installed system.

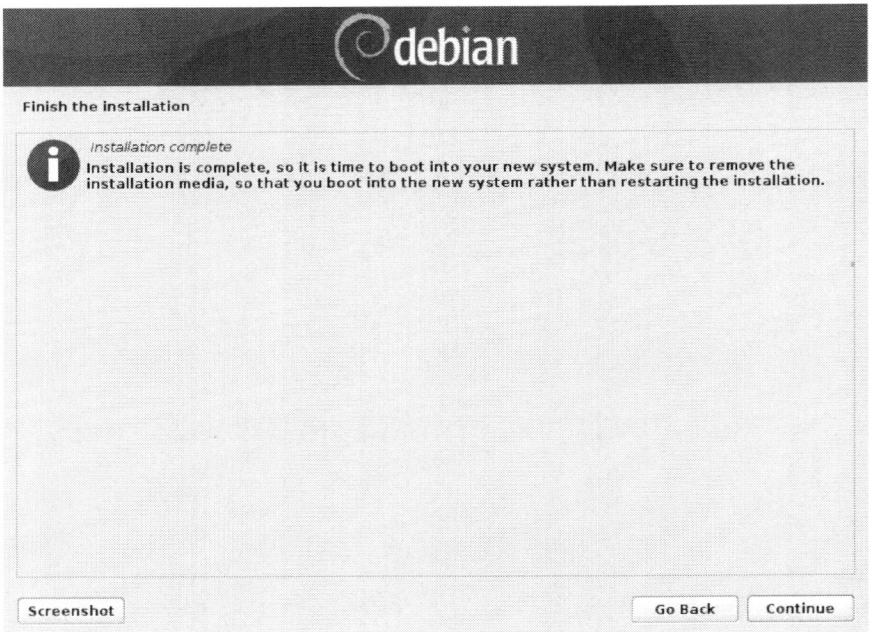

After a few seconds, the text-based GRUB boot menu will appear on the screen (see adjacent extract). The boot menu includes two options: *Debian GNU/Linux* and *Advanced options*

for Debian GNU/Linux. The first menu item is highlighted and pre-selected. The second menu entry allows you to set specific boot options. For a comprehensive list of these options have a look at the GNU GRUB manual at www.gnu.org/software/grub /manual/grub. Keep the first menu item selected and press Enter to proceed and boot the new system.

```
* Debian GNU/Linux
  Advanced options for Debian GNU/Linux
```

Your Debian system will start and initialize the necessary system services. This step will take a few seconds to be completed. Finally, a black-and-white screen will be visible on the first text terminal named *tty1* and ask you to log into the system. The login prompt consists of two components: the hostname of your Linux system (debian106) followed by a space and the word *login*.

```
Debian GNU/Linux 10 debian106 tty1

debian106 login: _
```

Having logged into the system you will be able to add further software to be able to use a graphical user interface, based on the XFCE desktop. At this step of the installation process, adding further software can only be done by logging in as the administrative root user.

To do so, type in *root* at the login prompt, press Enter, wait for the text *Password:* to appear and type in the password set for the root user you defined earlier. The Linux system will welcome you with a login message (see next page). The login message will display the version of the Linux kernel that is currently running and the usage advice.

Debian GNU/Linux 10 debian106 tty1

debian106 login: root
Password:
Linux debian106 4.19.0-11-amd64 #1 SMP Debian 4.19.146-1
(2020-09-17) x86_64

The programs included with the Debian GNU/Linux system
are free software; the exact distribution terms for each program are described in the individual files in
/usr/share/doc/*/copyright.

Debian GNU/Linux comes with ABSOLUTELY NO WAR-
RANTY, to the extent permitted by applicable law.

After this message, Debian opens a command-line prompt:

root@debian106 ~#_

This command-line prompt consists of four components:

root	The name of the user who logged in.
debian106	The hostname of the Linux system.
~	The current directory. In this case, it is the home directory of the user currently logged in. If not otherwise set, this is defined as /home/username for regular users and /root for the administrative user. ~ is just an abbreviation.
#	The login symbol. The # symbol represents the root user whereas $ is used by regular users without administrative rights. You will see this going forward when using various commands.

Important: You are now logged in as the administrative root user. Take care which commands you type in and check twice if in doubt. Any mistakes can lead to having to repair your Linux system.

Adding a Graphical User Interface

At its current stage, the Debian system is fully active and can be used as-is. For a desktop system suitable for a regular user, it still lacks a nice and easy-to-use graphical user interface to make it look and feel more familiar to the Windows or macOS systems you have gotten used to. In this step, we will change that and install the XFCE desktop manager. To do so, we will install the following packages:

- The aptitude package manager.
- The xdm display manager.
- The xfce4 desktop environment.

Debian uses the package manager **apt** to handle the installation, update, and removal of software packages and the related package lists. Also, **apt** resolves all the package dependencies and ensures that the relevant software is available on the system. In our case, roughly 170 MB of data has to be retrieved from the package mirror and installed. As pointed out earlier, this requires a working internet connection.

To install the three packages, type in the following commands at the command-line prompt. Just type the command after the # symbol:

```
root@debian106 ~# apt-get install aptitude xdm xfce4
```

apt will display further information regarding the packages to be installed. This includes the list of depending packages and recommended packages. At the end, you will see a command-line prompt. Type Y or press Enter to install Aptitude, xdm, and xfce4 as well as the depending packages. For the xdm display manager, two dialog boxes have to be confirmed. Press Enter on both to confirm the use of xdm.

The retrieval of the software packages to be installed takes a while. When finished, the command-line prompt will appear again. To activate the changes regarding the graphical desktop environment, restart the system. Type the command **reboot** at the command-line prompt as follows:

```
root@debian106 ~# reboot
```

Having restarted the Linux system, Debian welcomes us with a graphical boot screen (see below). Press Enter to start the Linux system with the default settings.

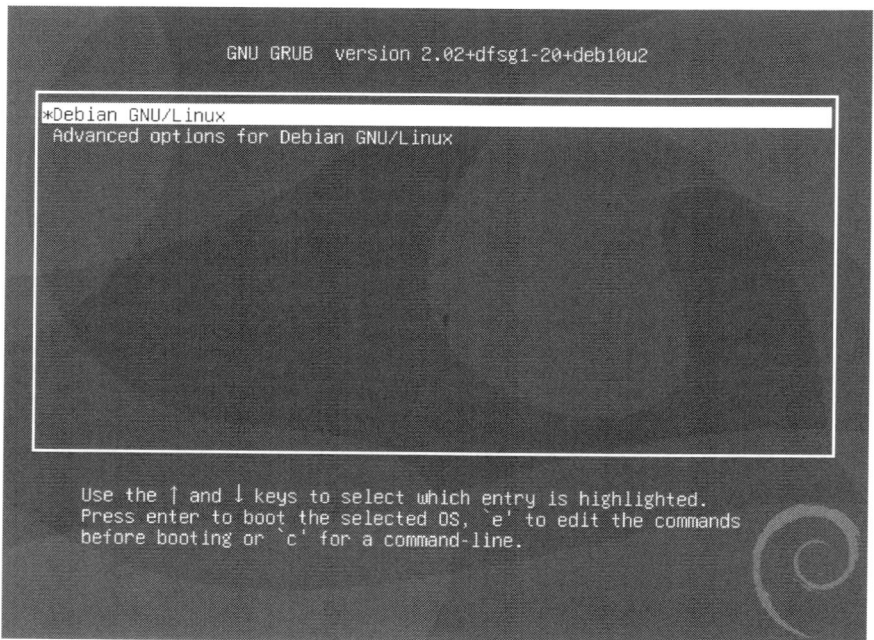

A few seconds later a graphical login screen will be visible. Log in to the system with the regular user named *user* as created earlier. Type in *user*, press Enter and type in the password for the user. Then, press Enter again to confirm and log in.

Next, the XFCE desktop will be visible (see below). The desktop comes with several default elements: an upper navigation bar, a lower navigation bar, and desktop icons. These elements are explained in more detail below.

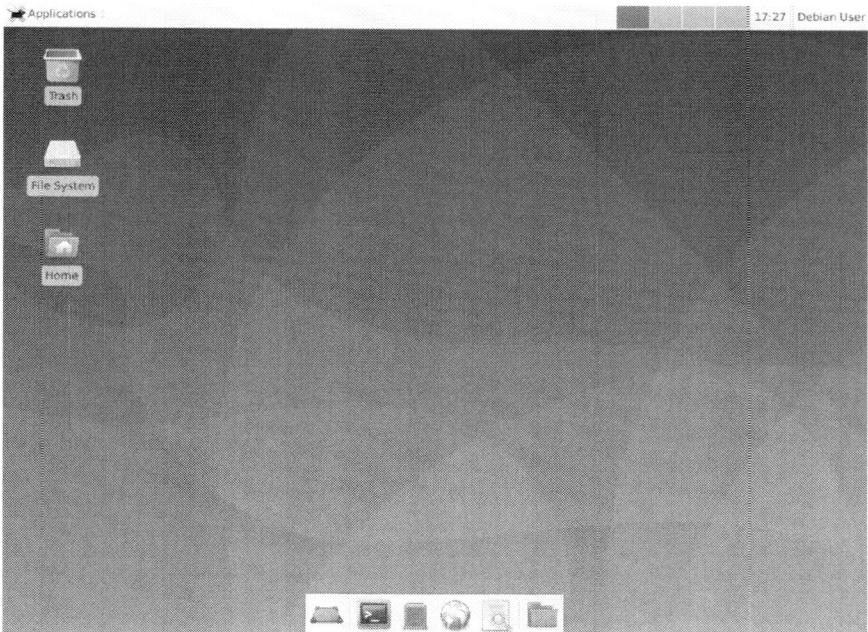

Upper navigation bar

This shows buttons to access the different applications, the four virtual desktop screens, the clock, and a button for various user actions such as to lock the screen, change the user, change to standby mode, and exit the current session.

Lower navigation bar

This bar contains several buttons to hide all the opened windows and show the empty desktop, to open a terminal, the file manager, a web browser, to find an application, and to open the file manager directly.

Desktop icons

From top to bottom there is a trash bin, file manager icons that link to the computer, and the home directory.

A right-click on the desktop opens a context menu that allows you to access the various applications (see below).

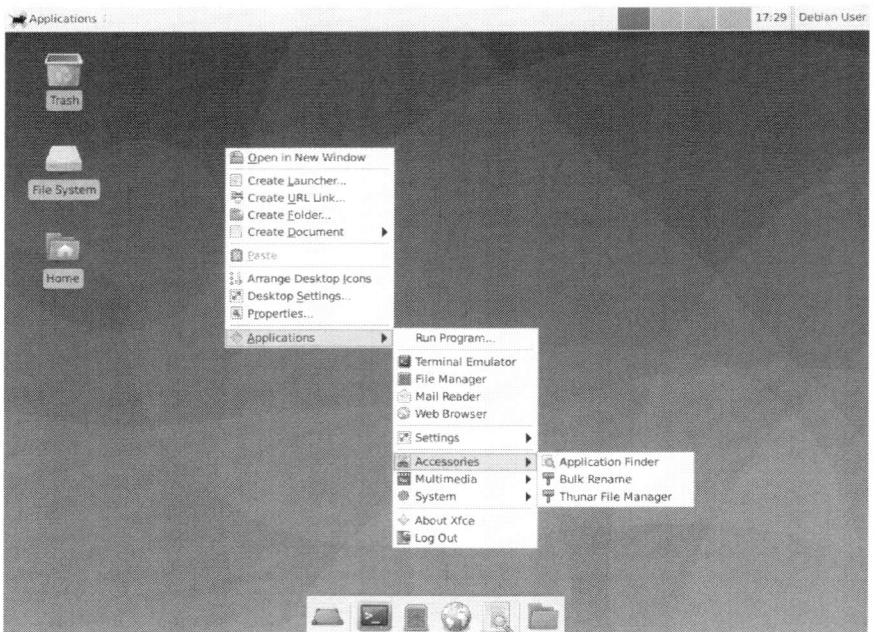

Adding Additional Packages

Up until now the software available to be used on your Linux system has been rather limited. The next thing to do is to add some functionality with these four Debian packages:

firefox-esr   The web browser Mozilla Firefox (Extended Support Release).

gnome-terminal   A terminal emulation maintained by the GNOME project.

xscreensaver   A basic screensaver for the X11 system.

vlc   The VLC video player.

The installation of the three packages will be done using the command-line in a terminal emulator (we will look at terminals in detail later in the guide). Currently on your system, the X11 terminal emulator *xterm* is installed. To open xterm, click on the terminal button in the lower navigation bar or select the entry Application > System > Xterm from the context menu.

As step one, open xterm. Next, type in the command **su** next to the command-line prompt as follows and press Enter:

```
user@debian106: ~$ su
Password:
```

You may remember from the previous steps that only an administrative user can install, update, or remove software on a Debian system. The **su** command abbreviates *switch user* and changes your current role. Used without an additional name, the role changes to the administrative root user. At the password prompt type in the password for the administrative user and press Enter.

As an administrative user, install the packages: firefox-esr, gnome-terminal, xscreenserver, and vlc as follows, with the output shown thereafter.

> root@debian106: ~# apt-get install firefox-esr gnome-terminal xscreensaver vlc

After the installation of the four packages, you can switch back to your role as a regular user. Press Ctrl+D to quit the admin part, and press Ctrl+D again to close xterm. The installation of Firefox has the following effects:

- The new software *Firefox* is available from the application menu.

- The new command **firefox** is available from the command-line.
- The earth icon from the lower navigation bar links to the Firefox web browser.
- The installation of the GNOME terminal package has the following effects:
- The new software *gnome-terminal* is available from both the command-line and the application menu.
- The terminal icon from the lower navigation bar links to the GNOME terminal.
- The entry *Open Terminal Here* from the context menu refers to the GNOME terminal.

To see the changes, select the entry *Open Terminal Here* from the context menu. The image below shows the terminal window. It comes with a white background and a bigger font that is easier to read.

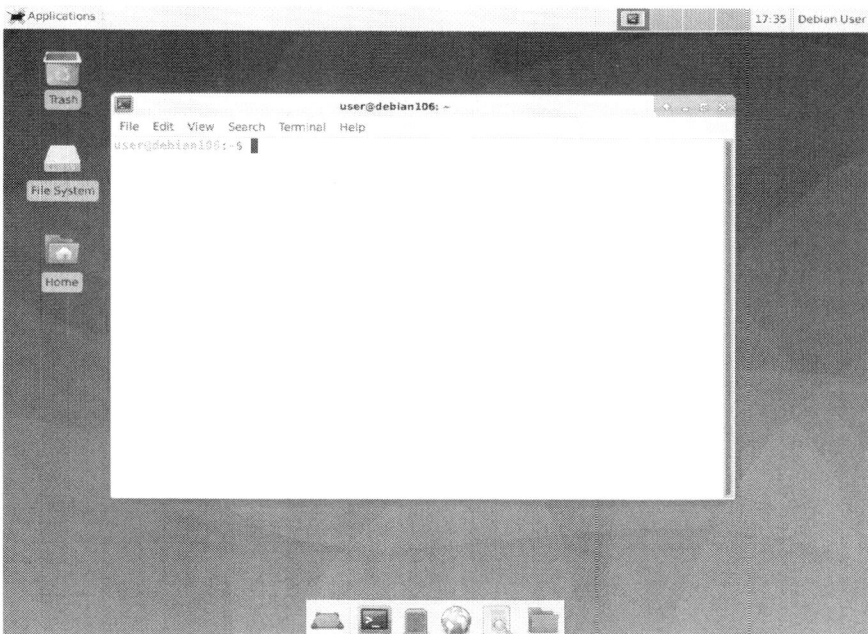

Exiting Linux

To use Linux properly, you also have to learn how to exit Linux and to reboot the system. Up next, you will learn how to quit the XFCE desktop environment, to shut down the Linux system, and to reboot the system. We will look at two methods, the first is based on the graphical interface and the second can be used on non-graphical systems like servers and wireless routers.

Quitting the XFCE Desktop Environment

The easiest way to quit the XFCE desktop and to log out from your current session is to click on the button in the right corner of the upper navigation bar. The button is labeled with your username, which in our case is *Debian User*. From the small menu select the last item labeled *Log Out*. Alternatively, you can choose either the item labeled *Log Out* from the Application button in the upper-left corner or from the context menu.

A second window opens that contains the five buttons labeled Log Out, Restart, Shutdown, Suspend, and Hibernate. Click on *Log Out* to quit your session. Subsequently, you will return to the login screen.

Shutting Down the Linux System

The way to shut down the entire Linux system is similar to exiting XFCE. Click on the button in the right corner of the upper navigation bar and select the *Shut Down*. From the next dialog window click on the button labeled *Shut Down* to stop the Linux system. From a terminal session, you can run the commands **halt** or **shutdown -h now** as an administrative user. A regular user is not allowed to issue these commands.

```
# halt
```

Rebooting the Linux System

To restart the Linux system, click on the button in the right corner of the upper navigation bar and select the item labeled *Restart*. From the next dialog window click on the button labeled *Restart* to reboot the Linux system. From a terminal session, you can run the command **reboot** or **shutdown -r now** as an administrative user. Again, a regular user is not allowed to issue these commands.

```
# reboot
```

Thumbs up or thumbs down?

I would love your feedback on the content and format of this guide, good or bad. I use your input to add more value to revisions of this guide and future guides. So let me know what you liked, and what you didn't like so far, through a short review on Amazon. My wife and I read each and every one of them.

a

## CHAPTER FIVE

Navigating Linux

F ilesystems on UNIX/Linux systems contain different types of entries. This includes regular files, directories (or folders), symbolic links, block and character devices, named pipes, and sockets. This chapter deals with directories and the corresponding Linux tools.

The Filesystem Hierarchy Standard (FHS)

Modern Linux systems have a rather consistent directory structure, which is based on the Filesystem Hierarchy Standard (FHS). This definition specifies which main directories exist, and which content is stored in them. The FHS is maintained by the Linux Foundation. The latest version of the FHS is 3.0 and was released back in 2015. The Linux distributions mentioned in Chapter 3 follow the FHS structure. Below are the common directories that are in use.

Common Directories

Directory	Description
/	Primary hierarchy root and root directory of the entire filesystem hierarchy

Directory	Description
/boot	The boot loader
/bin	Essential command binaries for all the users
/etc	Abbreviates etcetera and contains host-specific system-wide configuration files
/home	The home directories of the users
/lib	Libraries essential for the binaries in /bin and /sbin
/media	Mount points for removable media
/proc	Abbreviates processes and is the virtual filesystem of the Linux kernel
/root	The home directory for the root user
/sbin	Essential system binaries
/tmp	Temporary data and files
/usr	Unix System Resources, contains user utilities and applications
/var	Variable data, such as log and database files

Some Linux distributions have additional directories like /opt or use symbolic links. Linux also has some abbreviations in use, which can be quite helpful in your daily work.

Directory Abbreviations

Abbreviation	Description
$HOME	A local variable that contains the user's home directory
~	Points to the user's home directory like /home/tom
.	Points to the current directory
..	Points to the parent directory

You can use these abbreviations on the command line in a terminal and in shell scripts to shorten commands. Next, we will look at some of these commands.

Commands for Directories

As with files, Linux offers a range of commands to list, create, remove, change and rename directories. You can use these commands in your terminal.

Listing Directories

To list the directories, use the command **ls** with the switch **-d** (short for --directory) as follows:

```
$ ls -d */
finances/
projects/
work/
...
$
```

This example lists the names of the directories in the current directory. The dotted line (...) in the output indicates that the list is longer and the output is shortened here.

Two common ways of using the **ls** command are without any options and with the options **-la** (short for -l -a which means long all). The first output displays the entry names only for regular files, whereas the second output lists both regular and hidden entries. In order to list all the directories including the hidden ones starting with a period (.) use the **find** command as follows:

```
$ find . -maxdepth 1 -type d
./projects
```

```
./.mozilla
./.ipython
./.dbus
./video
...
$
```

The **tree** command searches the directory recursively and outputs an entire directory structure quite nicely. The switch **-d** limits the output to directories only and looks as follows:

```
$ tree -d
.
|———— archive
|  |———— ballet-zebola
|  |  |———— documents
|  |  |———— invoices
|  |———— charles-darwin-university
|———— projects
|———— .dbus
|———— .ipython
|———— .mozilla
...
$
```

Creating Directories

To create a directory, use the **mkdir** command (make directory). The next example creates a new entry named *training* in the current directory:

```
$ mkdir training
$
```

The switch **-v** (short for --verbose) prints an additional message that the command succeeded.

```
$ mkdir -v training
mkdir: directory "training" created
$
```

The switch **-p** (short for --parents) allows you to create entire subdirectory structures. Parent directories that do not exist yet are created as well. The following example creates the directory *training* as well as its subdirectories *linux* (level 1) and *lpic1* (level 2).

```
$ mkdir -p training/linux/lpic1
$
```

To create two subdirectories on the same level, make use of the underlying command line interpreter's capabilities. The Bash uses values in curly brackets { } to achieve this. The next example shows you how to create the two directories training/linux /lpic1 and training/linux/lpic2 in one go:

```
$ mkdir -p training/linux/{lpic1,lpic2}
$
```

Removing Directories

Removing a directory is done using the **rmdir** command (remove directory). The next example removes the entry named *training* in the current directory:

```
$ rmdir training
$
```

As with **mkdir,** the switch **-v** (short for --verbose) prints an additional message that the command succeeded.

```
$ rmdir -v training
mkdir: directory is removed, "training"
$
```

This works well, as long as the directory is empty. In case your directory contains any entries like files or subdirectories, the **rmdir** command will complain when using this message, and keep the directory unchanged:

```
$ rmdir training
rmdir: failed to remove `training': Directory not empty
$
```

To solve this situation the **rm** command (remove) combined with the switch **-r** (short for --recursive) becomes quite handy. Then, **rm** removes all the entries recursively. The following example combines the two switches **-r** and **-v** to delete one file and three directories.

```
$ tree training/
training/
|---- lpic1
|  |---- introduction.txt
|---- lpic2

2 directories, 1 file
$ rm -rv training/
„training/lpic1/introduction.txt" was removed
Directory was removed: „training/lpic1"
Directory was removed: „training/lpic2"
```

Directory was removed: „training/"
$

To be on the safe side when deleting files and directories, use the option -i (for --interactive) in combination with -v (for --verbose). Before deleting a file **rm** will then request your explicit confirmation, and prints a status message.

Changing Directories

The **cd** (change directory) command allows you to move through the system. To move one level upwards towards the root directory, use this command:

$ cd ..
$

To move downwards into a subdirectory, enter the **cd** command followed by the directory name. The command **cd /home/user/test** will take you straight into the /home /user/test directory.

As already explained earlier, there are some shortcuts available. The commands **cd ~** (tilde) and **cd $HOME** will always take you to your home directory whereas **cd /** will take you to the / directory.

Tip: Because Linux is case-sensitive, **cd** is not the same as **CD**. Be careful when using upper- and lower-case characters.

Renaming Directories

The **mv** command abbreviates the word *move,* and moves and renames files and directories. It requires two names: the name of the original file and its new name. To change the name of a directory from *lpic1* to *lpic-1* type in the following:

```
$ mv lpic1 lpic-1
$
```

The original file is removed and the new entry receives the current timestamp. Use the option **-i** (or --interactive) to prevent overwriting existing files.

Terminal-based File Managers

Navigating Linux on the command line is not the most ideal situation. Terminal-based and graphical file managers are a great alternative. Terminal-based file managers run inside a terminal and do not open a separate window on your desktop. There are tons of programs available, that's why we only present you with a selection of our favorites.

GNU Midnight Commander (mc)
www.midnight-commander.org

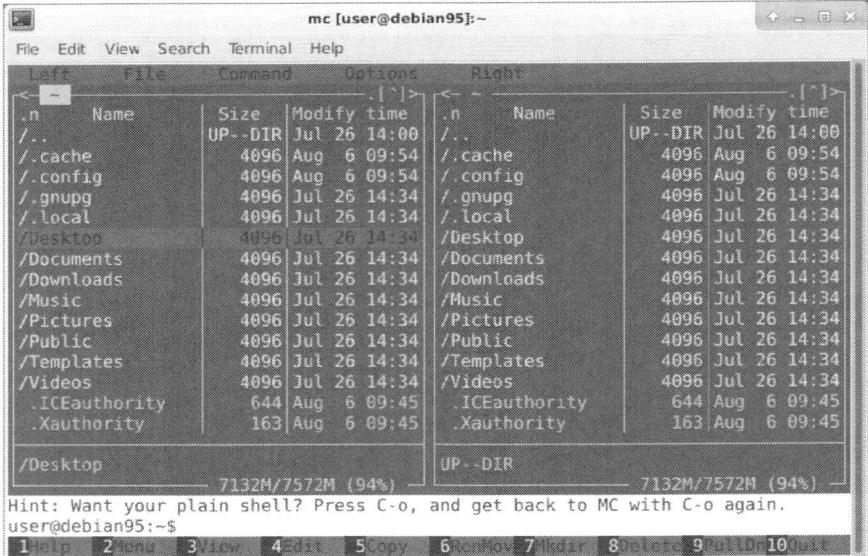

This is a free software, full-screen, text mode, visual file manager that lets you search, copy, move and also delete both single and multiple files, and even a whole directory tree. The mc integrates a viewer and editor.

The Vi File Manager (vifm)
https://vifm.info/

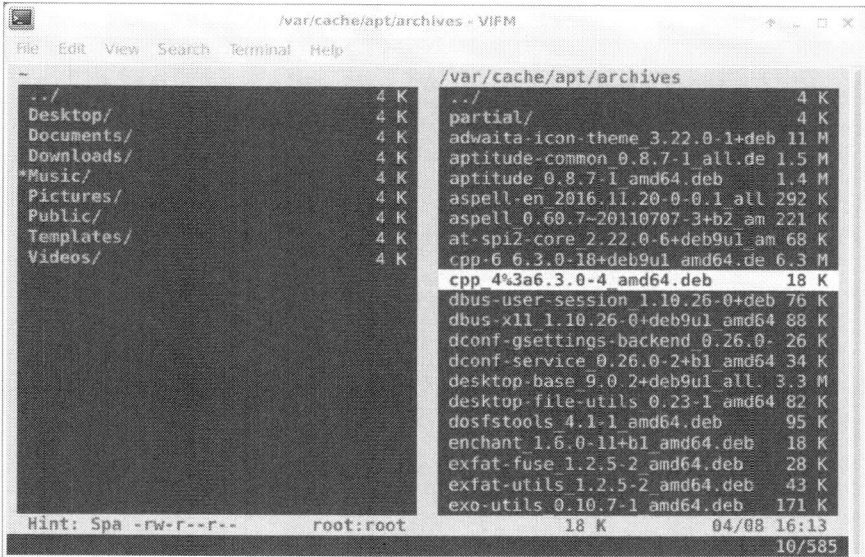

Similar to mc, the Vi File Manager (vifm) comes with two navigation windows based on a curses interface. It provides a Vi(m)-like environment for managing files and directories. If you are familiar with the Vi key bindings, this is the file manager for you.

Graphical File Managers

Similar to terminal-based file managers, graphical file managers assist in navigating Linux. These file managers do open in separate windows but provide a much nicer user experience.

Again, there are tons of programs available, so we only list our favorites below.

Konqueror
https://packages.debian.org/stretch/konqueror

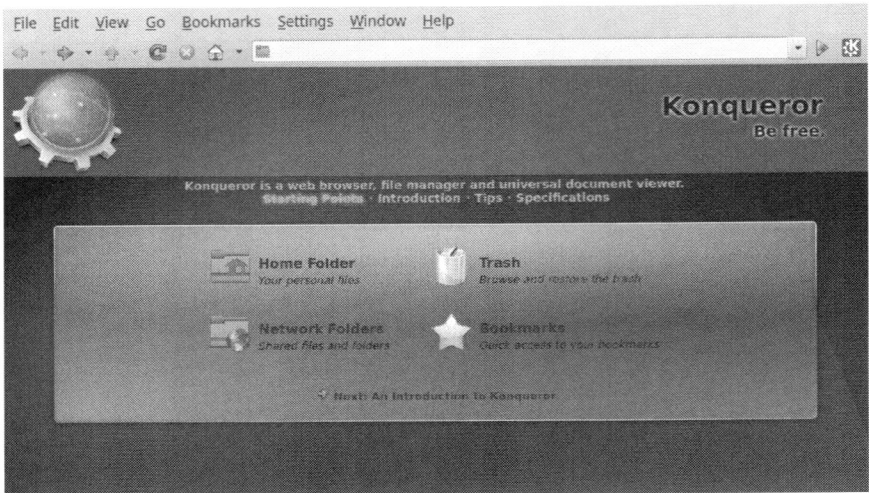

Konqueror is a powerful file manager for the KDE desktop environment. Konqueror offers simple file management functionalities such as copying, moving, searching, and deleting files and directories, plus some advanced features and functionalities such as access to archives, browse and rip audio CDs, and support for access to FTP and SFTP servers and SAMBA (Windows) shares.

Nautilus
https://wiki.gnome.org/Apps/Nautilus

Nautilus is the file manager on the GNOME desktop. It offers easy navigation and management of files on a Linux system. This includes simple file management functionalities such as copying, moving, searching, and deleting files and directories, as well as easy access to local and remote files.

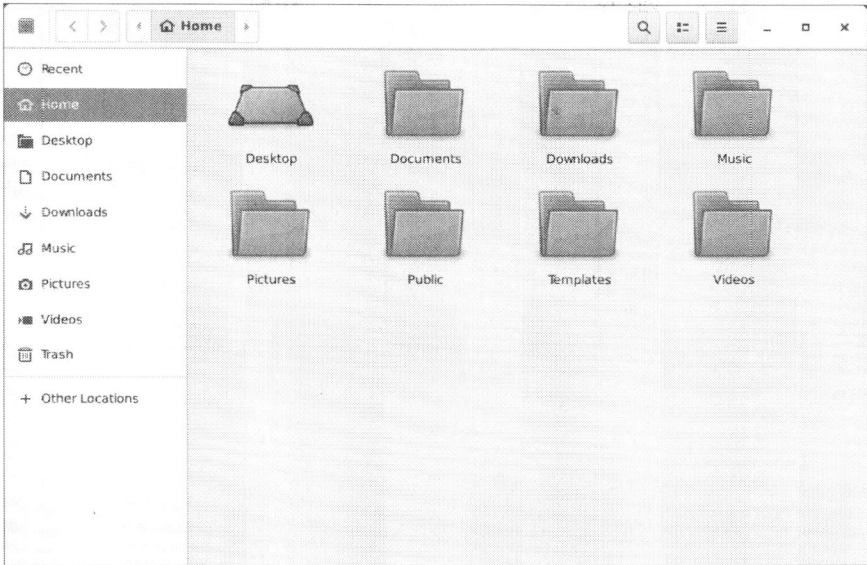

Dolphin
www.kde.org/applications/system/dolphin/

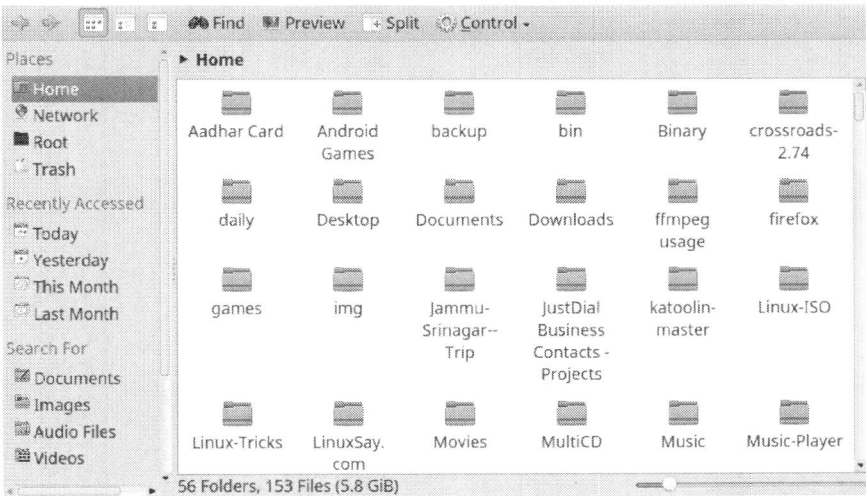

Dolphin is a lightweight file manager developed as part of the KDE applications package. Designed for simplicity, flexibility, and full customization, it allows users to browse, locate, open, copy, and move files around a Linux system with a lot of ease.

Thunar

https://docs.xfce.org/xfce/thunar/start

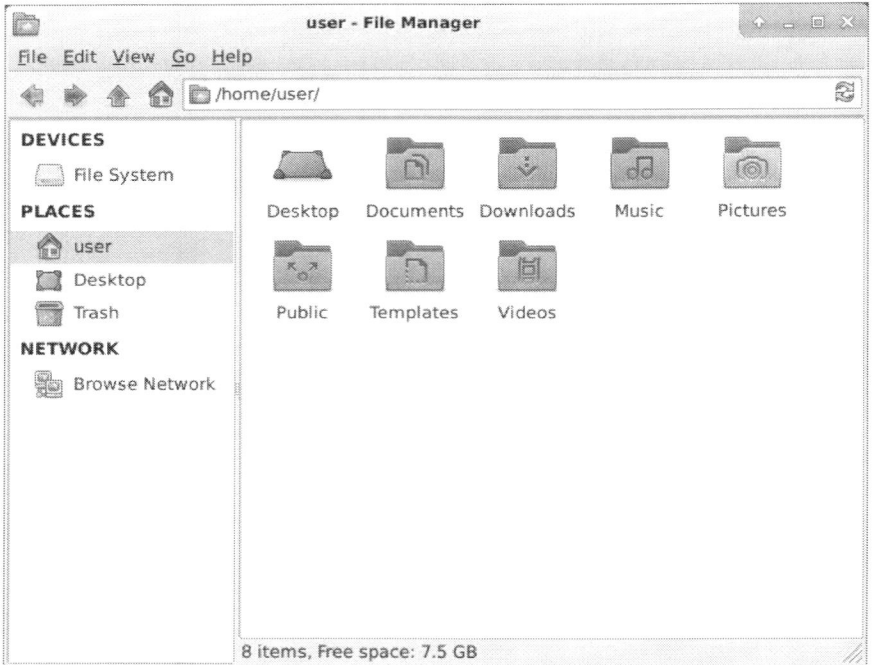

Thunar is a modern, lightweight file manager for the XFCE desktop. It is designed to be fast, responsive, and easy to use. We list it here because it has a clean and intuitive interface with important user options available.

## CHAPTER SIX

Introduction to Terminals and Shells

Working with the Linux operating system requires you to know about the terminal and the command line. It is essential to know what these are and to be slightly familiar with their usage and the standard commands available. But don't fear, we will describe each in detail. These terms sound much more intimidating than they are in reality.

The ability to communicate with the system in a text-based format is one reason why programmers have a soft spot for Linux, as this is the normal way for programmers to give instructions to computers. Another reason is the absolute control this allows you over the system that other operating systems just cannot provide, even with their own command line interpreters.

Some beginners have even reported that using and becoming familiar with issuing commands in this text-based format has made the transition to program development much easier and quicker.

What is a Terminal?

A terminal is described as "a program that emulates a video terminal within some other display architecture. Though typically synonymous with a *shell* or text terminal, the term *terminal* covers all remote terminals, including graphical interfaces. A terminal emulator inside a graphical user interface is often called a terminal window". To be precise, a terminal is simply the outer software. Inside a terminal runs a command line interpreter that is called a *shell*. The terminal is your way of interacting with the *shell* via a GUI.

Debian supports a long list of terminal software. This includes the Aterm, as well as the GNOME terminal, the Kterm, the Mate Terminal, the Rxvt, the Xterm, and the Xvt. These different implementations of terminal software vary in terms of stability, support for character sets, design, colors and fonts, as well as the possibility to apply background images or work with transparency.

In this book, we will use the GNOME terminal because of its stability, simplicity, and adjustability. To increase and decrease the size of the content that is displayed inside the terminal window, use the two-key combinations CTRL+ and CTRL-.

What is a Shell?

Simply speaking, a shell is a sophisticated command-line interpreter. The shell reads your commands, modifies them under certain conditions, and then executes the result. Between reading from the command-line and the execution of the actual result, the shell has to interpret special characters that are part of your input. The table below displays the available special characters.

Command Line Special Characters

Character	Meaning
$name	Substitution of a variable
name=	Assignment of a variable
'command'	Substitution of a command
$(command)	Substitution of a command
< > >> 2> 2>>	Redirection of input and output
|	Pipelining of commands
" ' \	Quoting
* [ ] ?	Creation of file names (globbing)
;	Separation of commands
&	Run the command in the background
|| &&	Run the commands under certain conditions
{ } ( )	Cramp commands

Purely for interest, the shell divides the command-line into single words to determine the commands, through the following process.

Shell Sequence

Step	Description	Special Characters
1	Read until the command separator and tagging (substitution of commands)	\n & | || && ; $(...) \ "..." '...'
2	Tagging (input-/output redirection, assignment of values)	< > >> 2> 2>> name=
3	Division into single words	space, tabulator

Step	Description	Special Characters
4	Substitution of variables	$name
5	Substitution of commands	tagging, see step 1 and 2
6	Input-/output redirection	tagging, see step 1 and 2
7	Assignment of variables	tagging, see step 1 and 2
8	Division into words	based on IFS
9	Creation of file names	* [-]
10	Command execution	

In steps 1 and 2, tagging happens for steps 5 to 7 only, and no further action takes place. Steps 5 to 7 are executed if tagging is completed. Next, the shell removes all the special characters. In step 10 the command-line contains only the arguments that are needed to execute the command. The shell interprets the first word as the name of the command to be executed, and the remaining words are its arguments:

```
command arg1 arg2 arg3 ...
```

Available Shells

Your Linux system allows the usage of various shells. Each shell is available as a separate software package through the Debian package manager, *Aptitude*, we installed earlier. The list of shells is quite long, so we list only a selection of the available shells that are the most popular:

- Almquist Shell (ash)
- Bourne Again Shell (bash)
- Debian Almquist Shell (dash)
- Z Shell (zsh)
- C Shell (csh)

- Korn Shell (ksh)
- Tenex C Shell (tcsh)

Unless otherwise stated, the examples in this guide are based on the Bourne Again Shell (bash). At the time of writing this is the default shell on Debian. Which other shells are allowed in your Linux system, is set up in the configuration file /etc/shells. Using the **cat** command, you can see the list of allowed shells. **cat** will be discussed in detail in Chapter 7. For now, know that the command simply outputs the contents of a file to the screen.

```
$ cat /etc/shells
# /etc/shells: valid login shells
/bin/sh
/bin/dash
/bin/bash
/bin/rbash
/usr/bin/screen
$
```

The name of the shell that is currently in use in the terminal, is kept in the shell variable named $0. The following simple command outputs the shell's name:

```
$ echo $0
bash
$
```

To change the shell that is currently in use, have a look at the configuration file /etc/passwd and the **chsh** command covered in Chapter 10.

Shell Scripting

At first glance, a shell script may sound daunting but it is quite straightforward. In the simplest form, it is just a sequence of UNIX/Linux commands that are stored in a file, and are executed line-by-line by the command line interpreter. A shell script is similar to typing single commands in the terminal, but they are executed as a batch. This makes it much faster and helps to automate tasks. For this guide, we will not be delving into the programming intricacies of shell scripting. But it is worth noting the recommended structure of a shell script.

Shebang Line

The shebang line defines which program will be used to properly process the instructions that follow the shebang line. The line starts with a #! which is a two-byte number indicating that the following lines are an executable shell script. The shebang is followed by the path to the interpreter or program that is to process the instructions.

Docstring

This is a short description of what the script does and the software license of the code. This can be a single line but also an extensive description. Such lines start with a # and are treated as comments by the shell.

Commands

This refers to the combination of single commands that are to be executed by the shell. As mentioned, this can be as little as a one-line instruction such as what we have in our example below, to a fully-fledged program.

Exit state

The exit state defines the return value(s) of the script. Unless explicitly stated otherwise, the exit state of the last command executed in the script will be returned. It is common to return 0 on success and a value between 1 and 255 in the event of an error.

The following basic script contains all the single elements we mentioned above. The purpose of the script is to determine the uptime of the computer.

```
#!/bin/bash
# determine the uptime of the system
# Released under GNU Public License (GPL)
uptime
# define exit state: no error
exit 0
```

There are two ways to execute a shell script. We can either call a shell such as Bash to run it or set the executable flag for the script and run it afterward. The first option uses Bash and looks as follows:

```
$ bash uptime.sh
12:20:31 up 7 days, 2:09, 6 users, load average: 0,74, 0,40, 0,27
$
```

The second method is based on two steps. First, we set the executable flag for the script using the **chmod** command:

```
$ chmod u+x uptime.sh
$
```

Then we can run the script:

```
$ ./uptime.sh
12:26:07 up 7 days, 2:14, 6 users, load average: 0,23, 0,34, 0,28
$
```

## CHAPTER SEVEN

Text Processing

L inux runs on text files for the most part. For example, the configuration files that are stored in /etc are stored as text files. Linux offers a rich set of text processing commands that are quite comprehensive and also time-saving. Knowing what they are and how they work will play a vital role in many of the upcoming chapters that delve deeper into Linux. In this chapter, we will have a look at these commands and show how to use them.

Text Processing Commands

cat

Short for concatenate, **cat** outputs the contents of a file to the screen or standard output. The command **cat /etc/passwd** will output all the lines of the file /etc/passwd to the screen.

```
$ cat /etc/passwd
root:x:0:0:root:/root:/bin/bash
daemon:x:1:1:daemon:/usr/sbin:/usr/sbin/nologin
bin:x:2:2:bin:/bin:/usr/sbin/nologin
sys:x:3:3:sys:/dev: /usr/sbin/nologin
```

```
sync:x:4:65534:sync:/bin:/bin/sync
games:x:5:60:games:/usr/games:/usr/sbin/nologin
man:x:6:12:man:/var/cache/man:/usr/sbin/nologin
lp:x:7:7:lp:/var/spool/lpd:/usr/sbin/nologin
mail:x:8:8:mail:/var/mail:/usr/sbin/nologin
news:x:9:9:news:/var/spool/news:/usr/sbin/nologin
uucp:x:10:10:uucp:/var/spool/uucp:/usr/sbin/nologin
proxy:x:13:13:proxy:/bin:/usr/sbin/nologin
www-data:x:33:33:www-data:/var/www:/usr/sbin/nologin
backup:x:34:34:backup:/var/backups:/usr/sbin/nologin
list:x:38:38:Mailing List Manager:/var/list:/usr/sbin/nologin
irc:x:39:39:ircd:/var/run/ircd:/usr/sbin/nologin
....
$
```

cat can also write to a text file using the redirect operator (>). To do this, simply use the redirect operator and the name of your text file. For example:

```
cat > output.txt
```

Follow this by the lines of text you wish to output. To quit, press **Ctrl+D**, and type **cat output.txt** to see the result.

```
$ cat > output.txt
hello world
this is a test
to see if cat works
$ cat output.txt
hello world
this is a test
to see if cat works
$
```

Other useful options for **cat** are:

-E   Short for --show-ends. Outputs a $ at the end of each line.

-n   Short for --number. Numbers all output lines.

-s   Short for --squeeze-blank. Suppresses repeated empty output lines.

The **cat** command can also output multiple files at once. The command **cat /etc/passwd /etc/group** will output the contents of /etc/passwd and /etc/group. Keep in mind that the original files are not affected. The next example below outputs the contents of the file *output.txt* twice and continuously numbers all the output lines using the option **-n**.

```
$ cat -n output.txt output.txt
     1      hello world
     2      this is a test
     3       to see if cat works
     4      hello world
     5      this is a test
     6      to see if cat works
$
```

For a more substantial example, we are going to create three text files named *file1*, *file2,* and *file3*. Use the commands **cat > file1, cat > file2** and **cat > file3** to create the files. Do not forget to press **Ctrl+D** to exit and use the command **cat file1 file2 file3** to see them all at once.

```
$ cat > file1
this is file one
```

```
$ cat > file2
this is file two
$ cat > file3
this is file three
$ cat file1 file2 file3
this is file one
this is file two
this is file three
$
```

Using the redirect operator, we can then write all three files to a single file.

```
$ cat file1 file2 file3 > bigfile
$ cat bigfile
this is file one
this is file two
this is file three
$
```

tac

The **tac** command works in the same manner as the **cat** command but displays the lines in reverse order. Using *bigfile* from the previous section, let's display the file using **tac**:

```
$ tac bigfile
this is file three
this is file two
this is file one
$
```

more

While **cat** and **tac** display the entire file at once, **more** lets you view the file one screen at a time. Let's say we have a large text file named *alice.txt*. To view it type the following:

$ more alice.txt

This shows a screen of text starting at the beginning of the file. Use the spacebar to scroll through the pages. Alternatively, hitting Enter scrolls down one line at a time. The disadvantage of the **more** command is that it can only scroll down but not back up again. For that, there is the **less** command.

Chapter One - Down the Rabbit Hole: Alice a girl of seven years, is feeling bored and drowsy while sitting on the riverbank with her elder sister. She then notices a talking, clothed White Rabbit with a pocket watch run past. She follows it down a rabbit hole when suddenly she falls a long way to a curious hall with many locked doors of all sizes. She finds a small key to a door too small for her to fit through, but through it, she sees an attractive garden. She then discovers a bottle on a table labeled "DRINK ME", the contents of which cause her to shrink too small to reach the key which she has left on the table. She eats a cake with "EAT ME" written on it in currants as the chapter closes.

less

The **less** command is a terminal pager that displays one screen of text at a time and allows scrolling forward and backward in a file, but it cannot edit a file. Inside **less**, there are commands to traverse the file and to find certain patterns. Some examples are:

- j - go down one line.
- k - go up one line.
- g or < - go to the first line.
- G or > - go to the last line.
- <n>G - go to line <n>.
- Space - go to the next page.
- d - go forward half a page.
- b - go to the previous page.
- u - go back half a page.
- v - open page in the editor set by the VISUAL environment variable.
- /<regex> - search forward for <regex>.
- ?<regex> - Search backward for <regex>.
- n - next instance of text matching <regex>.
- N - previous instance of text matching <regex>.
- :n - next file when multiple files are opened in the same command.
- :p - previous file when multiple files are opened in the same command.
- q - quit.

head

This command outputs the first n-number of lines of a file. If n is not specified, it defaults to ten. The example below shows the default use of **head** for the file /etc/passwd.

```
$ head /etc/passwd
root:x:0:0:root:/root:/bin/bash
daemon:x:1:1:daemon:/usr/sbin:/usr/sbin/nologin
bin:x:2:2:bin:/bin:/usr/sbin/nologin
sys:x:3:3:sys:/dev: /usr/sbin/nologin
sync:x:4:65534:sync:/bin:/bin/sync
games:x:5:60:games:/usr/games:/usr/sbin/nologin
man:x:6:12:man:/var/cache/man:/usr/sbin/nologin
```

lp:x:7:7:lp:/var/spool/lpd:/usr/sbin/nologin
mail:x:8:8:mail:/var/mail:/usr/sbin/nologin
news:x:9:9:news:/var/spool/news:/usr/sbin/nologin
$

To output the first six lines of the file /etc/passwd, type this instead:

$ head -n6 /etc/passwd
root:x:0:0:root:/root:/bin/bash
daemon:x:1:1:daemon:/usr/sbin:/usr/sbin/nologin
bin:x:2:2:bin:/bin:/usr/sbin/nologin
sys:x:3:3:sys:/dev: /usr/sbin/nologin
sync:x:4:65534:sync:/bin:/bin/sync
games:x:5:60:games:/usr/games:/usr/sbin/nologin
$

The opposite of **head** is **tail** which we will explain next.

tail

The **tail** command outputs the last *n*-number of lines of a file. If *n* is not specified, it defaults to ten lines. The example below displays the last 5 lines of the file /etc/passwd.

$ tail -n5 /etc/passwd
usbmux:x:109:46:usbmux dae-
mon,,,:/var/lib/usbmux:/bin/false
pulse:x:110:114:PulseAudio dae-
mon,,,:/var/run/pulse:/bin/false
lightdm:x:111:116:Light Display Manager:/var/lib/lightdm:/bin/false
felix:x:1001:1001:Felix,,,:/home/felix:/bin/bash
caro:x:1002:1002:Caro,,,:/home/caro:/bin/bash
$

In addition, **tail** can be used to follow the progress of a log file by using **-f** (or --follow). As more data gets appended to the end of the file, the output on the screen updates. To output the progress of the last 20 lines of /var/log/syslog as it updates, use the following command:

```
$ tail -f -n 20 /var/log/syslog
```

sort

As the name implies, this command is used to sort files. Among others it has the following options:

-R   Random sort.

-r   Reverse the sort order.

-n   Sort numerically.

To sort the first five lines of the file /etc/passwd in alphabetical order, use this command:

```
$ head -n5 /etc/passwd | sort
bin:x:2:2:bin:/bin:/usr/sbin/nologin
daemon:x:1:1:daemon:/usr/sbin:/usr/sbin/nologin
root:x:0:0:root:/root:/bin/bash
sync:x:4:65534:sync:/bin:/bin/sync
sys:x:3:3:sys:/dev:/usr/sbin/nologin
$
```

Use the option **-r** to reverse the sort order:

```
$ head -n5 /etc/passwd | sort -r
sys:x:3:3:sys:/dev:/usr/sbin/nologin
sync:x:4:65534:sync:/bin:/bin/sync
root:x:0:0:root:/root:/bin/bash
```

```
daemon:x:1:1:daemon:/usr/sbin:/usr/sbin/nologin
bin:x:2:2:bin:/bin:/usr/sbin/nologin
$
```

uniq

This command reports or removes duplicate lines from a sorted file. Among others, it has the following options:

-c   Short for --count. Outputs the frequency of occurrence for each line.

-d   Short for --repeated. Reports the lines that occur more than once.

-u   Short for --unique. Reports the lines that appear only once.

The example below shows the basic usage of **uniq**. The output contains each line that only occurs once.

```
$ cat names.sorted
Greg      1967
John      1986
John      1986
Kate      1948
Pete      1977
$ uniq names.sorted
Greg      1967
John      1986
Kate      1948
Pete      1977
$
```

cut

The **cut** command extracts specified fields from files. It requires a delimiter in order to detect the field boundaries. The next example displays the name and the user ID from the file /etc/passwd. These are the first and third fields from each line (option **-f**), and the fields are separated by a colon (option **-d**).

```
$ cut -d":" -f1,3 /etc/passwd
...
colord:108
saned:109
usbmux:110
geoclue:111
sshd:112
uuidd:113
pulse:114
rtkit:115
avahi:116
...
$
```

tr

The idea behind this command is to translate, to substitute, and to delete characters from a string. **tr** reads from *stdin* and outputs to *stdout*. It has the following options:

-d   Short for --delete. Deletes the given characters from the string.

-s   Short for --squeeze-repeats. Replaces repeated characters with a single occurrence.

-t   Short for --truncate-set1. Truncates the given set of characters.

The first example shown below demonstrates how to convert lower case to upper case characters. **tr** accepts two sets of characters: the originals and the replacements. The number of characters in both sets must be the same.

```
$ cat bigfile
this is file one
this is file two
this is file three
$ cat bigfile | tr [a-z] [A-Z]
THIS IS FILE ONE
THIS IS FILE TWO
THIS IS FILE THREE
$
```

The second example demonstrates how to replace repeated spaces with a single one. A *space* is defined as a group of characters, being spaces, tabulators, carriage return, or linefeed.

```
$ echo "tools for     developers" | tr -s [:space:]
tools for developers
$ echo "tools for     developers" | tr -s [:space:] "-"
tools-for-developers
$
```

diff

This tool analyzes two files and prints the lines that are different. Moreover, **diff** outputs a description of which steps are needed to transform the first file into the second file. The example shown next demonstrates this for two files. The output line *1c1* means that the *first* line of file1 has to be changed to get the *first* line of file2. Below that is the referenced lines from the two files separated by dashes.

```
$ cat file1
this is file one
with a second line
$ cat file2
this is file two
with a second line
$ diff file1 file2
1c1
< this is file one
---
> this is file two
$
```

nl

nl is similar to **cat** (discussed earlier in this chapter) but adds a line number at the beginning of each line of output.

```
$ nl places
     1 Amsterdam
     2 Berlin
     3 Bern
     4 Cape Town
$
```

wc

This command abbreviates the phrase *word count* and respectively counts lines, words, and single characters of the input data. Unless otherwise specified, all three values are printed:

```
$ wc places
 4  5 32 places
$
```

Amongst others **wc** offers the following options to limit the output:

-l   Outputs the number of lines only, followed by the filename.

-w   Outputs the number of words only, followed by the filename.

-c   Outputs the number of characters only, followed by the filename.

This example shows how to count only the lines in a file:

```
$ wc -l places
4 places
$
```

Introduction to grep

The command-line tool **grep** is one of the most essential and powerful Linux commands, so much so that authors have written entire guides solely dedicated to it. **grep** acts as a filter and abbreviates the description of *global regular expression print*.

The command works on text data as a filter and only prints the lines of text that match a given pattern. **grep** requires data to work on, in combination with a pattern to look for. In this context, data refers to a series of characters that can come from *stdin* or a file, and a pattern can be formulated as a series of characters or as a regular expression. Four different pattern styles are supported by **grep**:

-G   Short for --basic-regexp. The pattern is formulated as a basic regular expression. This is the default case.

-F   Short for --fixed-strings. The pattern is not a regular expression and is interpreted as a fixed string instead. Can also be abbreviated as fgrep.

-P   Short for --perl-regexp. Rhe pattern is interpreted as a regular expression following Perl syntax.

-E   Short for --extended-regexp. The pattern is formulated as an extended regular expression that allows an added character set. Can also be abbreviated as egrep.

The number of options **grep** offers is quite extensive. The following is a list of the most notable options available:

-c   Counts and prints the number of matches from the search, but does not print the matches themselves.

--color   Highlights the matches from the search.

-H   Short for --with-filename. Each line of output starts with the name of the file the match was found in.

-i   Ignores case-sensitivity and includes both lower and uppercase matches.

-l   Short for --files-with-matches. Prints only the filenames that match the search.

-L   Short for --files-without-matches. Prints only the filenames that did not match the search.

-n   Short for --line-number. Each line of output starts with the line number of the corresponding match in the file.

-v   Prints all lines that do not match the search pattern.

-r   Short for --recursive. Search recursively in a directory structure to include all subdirectories in the search.

These options will become clearer with the help of a few practical examples. First, we will search for the fixed string *Linux* in one or more AsciiDoc files (.adoc). The output consists of the lines that contain the pattern.

```
$ grep Linux *.adoc
The Linux Environment. First Steps
$
```

Next, we perform the same search but also output the filename and line number the pattern was found in. Each line of output starts with the name of the file followed by a colon (:), the line number, another colon, and then the line that matches the pattern. In our example, the pattern was found in line 1 of the file *introduction.adoc*.

```
$ grep -Hn Linux *.adoc
introduction.adoc:1:The Linux Environment. First Steps.
$
```

This time round, we will again search for the string *Linux* in one or more AsciiDoc files, but we will include both lowercase and uppercase characters in the search.

```
$ grep -i Linux *.adoc
The Linux Environment. First Steps.
include::what-about-linux/what-about-linux.adoc
include::linux-in-day-to-day-life/linux-in-day-to-day-life.adoc
include::navigating-linux/navigating-linux.adoc
```

```
include::using-the-linux-terminal/using-the-linux-
terminal.adoc
$
```

Next, we will reverse our search and only show the names of files that do not contain the pattern *Linux*.

```
$ grep -vrl Linux */*.adoc
acknowledgements/acknowledgements.adoc
getting-help/getting-help.adoc
linux-in-day-to-day-life/linux-in-day-to-day-life.adoc
navigating-linux/navigating-linux.adoc
preface/preface.adoc
references/references.adoc
setting-up-debian/setting-up-debian.adoc
software-licenses/software-licenses.adoc
using-the-linux-terminal/using-the-linux-terminal.adoc
what-about-linux/what-about-linux.adoc
x11/x11.adoc
$
```

Let's now look at a few examples that are slightly more complex. In this instance, we will make use of the **ls** command we've seen earlier in the guide and filter the output for a specific pattern range. More specifically, we will search for PDF documents that have the numbers 12 to 16 in the filename.

```
$ ls E*.pdf | egrep --color '1[2-6].pdf$'
E_20160012.pdf
E_20160013.pdf
E_20160014.pdf
E_20160015.pdf
E_20160016.pdf
$
```

For the next example, we will search all the TeX files in the current directory that contain the pattern *nanostation* (a product name) with either an uppercase or lowercase *n* at the beginning, and either an uppercase or lowercase *s* in the middle of the name.

```
$ egrep --color '[Nn]ano[Ss]tation' *.tex
B0047.tex:Ubiquiti NanoStation M2
B0057.tex:Ubiquiti Nanostation M2 Loco
B0092.tex:Ubiquiti Nanostation M5
$
```

Lastly, we list all the software packages that are no longer installed on the system but are still configured. Here we use the **dpkg** command, which you will learn more of in Chapter 14. In our example, it simply lists the installed packages and their status. The **grep** command then filters all the lines that start with the two characters *rc*, which stands *for removed and configured.*

```
$ dpkg -l | egrep '^rc'
rc doxygen-gui 1.8.8-5 amd64 GUI configuration tool for
doxygen
rc kdiff3 0.9.98-1 amd64 compares and merges 2 or 3 files or
directories
rc ktorrent 4.3.1-2+b1 amd64 BitTorrent client based on the
KDE platform
rc libacpi0 0.2-4 amd64 general purpose library for ACPI
...
$
```

Combining Commands

Linux commands on their own are already quite powerful, but you can boost their functionality even further by combining them using a pipe or redirecting the input/output. We will demonstrate how to achieve this next.

Piping

Piping (using the keyboard character | found above the \) is a way of connecting two or more commands in a chain. The output of one command is not sent to *stdout* but directly given as an input to the next command.

This direct connection between commands allows them to operate simultaneously and permits data to be transferred directly between them continuously, rather than having to pass it through temporary text files or the display screen. Pipes are unidirectional, in other words, data flows from left to right through the pipeline. The example below shows the two commands **cat** and **wc** being used to count the number of words in a file.

```
$ cat file2
this is file two
with a second line
$ cat file2 | wc -w
8
$
```

Redirection

Redirection is a feature in Linux that, when executing a command, can change the standard input/output devices. The basic workflow of any Linux command is that it takes an input and gives an output. The standard input (stdin) device is the keyboard, and the standard output (stdout) device is the screen.

With redirection, the standard input/output can be changed. You can read the processed data from a different input source, and output the result to a different place. Output redirection is indicated by the > and >> symbols, and input redirection by the < symbol:

- The > symbol sends the output to the given file by creating a new file. If the file already exists it will be entirely replaced.
- The >> symbol sends the output to the given file and appends it at the end.
- The < symbol reads from the given input source.

The first example below uses the >> operator and adds a third line of text at the end of an existing file.

```
$ echo "line 3" >> file2
$ cat file2
this is file two
with a second line
line 3
$
```

The second example goes one step further by redirecting the standard output to a device. The **cat** command reads the file *music.mp3* and sends the output to the device /dev/audio which is the audio device. If the sound configuration in your computer is correct, this command will play the music file.

```
$ cat music.mp3 > /dev/audio
```

The next example combines input and output redirection. The **wc** command reads the contents from *file2* and counts the words using the option -w. The output is then sent to *stdout* and appended as a new line using the >> operator to the file *statistics*.

```
$ cat file2
this is file two
with a second line
line 3
$
$ wc -w < file2
10
$ wc -w < file2 >> statistics
$ cat statistics
10
$
```

## CHAPTER EIGHT

The Linux Boot Process

We start by looking at the first process in all Linux systems, the boot process. Starting up a UNIX or Linux system is a complex multi-part process, which consists of the following high-level steps:

1. The Basic Input Output System (BIOS) executes the Master Boot Record (MBR). Newer systems use the Unified Extensible Firmware Interface (UEFI).
2. The MBR executes a boot loader, such as the Grand Unified Bootloader (GRUB) or the Linux Loader (LILO).
3. The boot loader then executes the Linux kernel.
4. The Linux kernel runs the *init* process via /sbin/init to start the operating system.
5. Init then executes *init.d* with *runlevels* or *systemd*.

These steps are explained in more detail next.

BIOS and UEFI

Either the BIOS or the UEFI is run when starting the computer. This software is delivered from a vendor-specific firmware memory chip on the computer's motherboard, specific to that motherboard. The BIOS or UEFI first performs some system integrity checks. Then it searches the hard drives, CD/DVD drives, USB drives, and the network in a pre-selected order and boots the first boot loader program it finds. This boot loader is then loaded into memory and takes control of the system. In simple terms, the BIOS or UEFI loads and executes the boot loader.

At startup there is usually an option to press F1, F2, F12, Escape or Delete to enter the BIOS or UEFI menu. The boot loader search sequence can be changed from here. Once changes are made, usually the F10 key saves the changes and restarts the system with the new settings.

With most modern systems, BIOS is no longer used and has been replaced by UEFI BIOS. UEFI BIOS is maintained by the Unified EFI Forum. Support for UEFI by Debian is part of the default setup. Compared to BIOS, UEFI has the following advantages:

- The ability to use large-capacity disks (over 2 Terabytes) with a GUID Partition Table (GPT).
- CPU-independent architecture.
- CPU-independent drivers.
- A flexible pre-OS environment that includes network capability.
- A modular design.
- Backward and forward compatibility.

To determine if a Debian system is booted via UEFI, check for the directory /sys/firmware/efi. If that directory exists, the system is running in UEFI mode. A system without UEFI will return the following:

```
$ ls /sys/firmware/efi
ls: cannot access /sys/firmware/efi: No such file or directory
$
```

MBR

The Master Boot Record (MBR) is located in the first sector of the bootable disk. Typically, this is either /dev/hda or /dev/sda. It contains all information about the logical partitions on the disk. The MBR is less than 512 bytes in size and has the following three components:

1. Primary boot loader info in the first 446 bytes.
2. Partition table info in the next 64 bytes.
3. MBR validation check (signature) in the last two bytes.

The MBR contains information about GRUB. So in simple terms, it loads and executes the GRUB boot loader. The contents of the MBR may be viewed by combining the two commands **dd** (disk dump) and **hexdump** from the *coreutils* package and *bsdmainutils* package in the following manner:

```
# dd if=/dev/sda bs=512 count=1 | hexdump -C
```

In the above code **dd** reads the contents of the first SCSI disk /dev/sda, block by block as chunks of 512 bytes. The option **count=1** limits this step to reading the first block only. Then the output of **dd** is piped to **hexdump** using the option -C. The output of **hexdump** is shown as ASCII characters. The example on the following page illustrates this in more detail.

```
# dd if=/dev/sda bs=512 count=1 | hexdump -C
00000000    eb 63 90 10 8e d0 bc 00    b0 b8 00 00
00000010    fb be 00 7c bf 00 06 b9    00 02 f3 a4
00000020    00 be be 07 38 04 75 0b    83 c6 10 81
00000030    f3 eb 16 b4 02 b0 01 bb    00 7c b2 80
00000040    4c 02 cd 13 ea 00 7c 00    oo eb fe 00
00000050    00 00 00 00 00 00 00 00    00 00 00 80
00000060    00 00 00 00 ff fa 90 90    f6 c2 80 74
00000070    74 02 b2 80 ea 79 7c 00    00 31 c0 8e
00000080    00 20 fb a0 64 7c 3c ff    74 02 88 c2
00000090    f6 07 03 74 06 be 88 7d    e8 17 01 be
000000a0    bb aa 55 cd 13 5a 52 72    3d 81 fb 55
000000b0    e1 01 74 32 31 c0 89 44    04 40 88 44
000000c0    c7 04 10 00 66 8b 1e 5c    7c 66 89 5c
000000d0    60 7c 66 89 5c 0c c7 44    06 00 70 b4
...
```

The **dd** command can also be used to create a backup of the MBR as shown below. The output file is mbr.bin and is specified using the option **of=mbr.bin**, where *of* abbreviates from *output file*.

```
# dd if=/dev/sda bs=512 count=1 of=mbr.bin
1+0 records in
1+0 records out
512 bytes copied, 0.000371249 s, 1.4MB/s
# file mbr.bin
mbr.bin: DOS/MBR boot sector
#
```

GRUB

The software that handles the Linux startup is called the *Grand Unified Bootloader* (GRUB), or GNU GRUB to be precise. Its function is to take over from the BIOS at boot time, load itself, load the Linux kernel into memory, and then turn over execution to the Linux kernel. Once the kernel takes over, GRUB has done its job and is no longer needed.

Note that GRUB version 1 has been replaced by GRUB2, the former is now referred to as GRUB Legacy. For simplicity, GRUB2 is simply called GRUB.

At boot time, GRUB displays a splash screen and presents a menu from which to start the system. The more Linux kernel images present on the system, the longer the list of entries. The image below shows the default installation with two menu entries. Unless stated otherwise, the first menu points to the default entry.

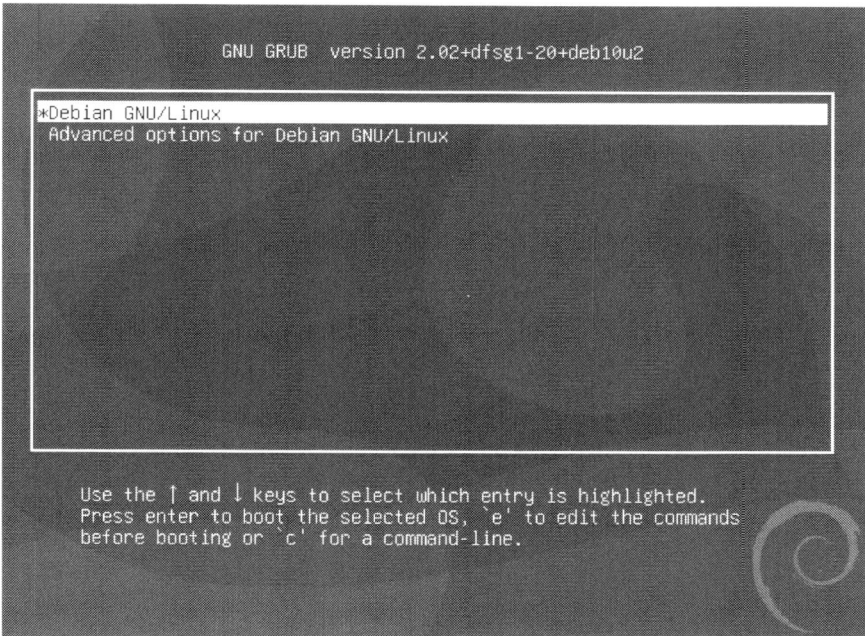

GRUB waits for a few seconds, then loads the kernel image selected from the menu. The first entry targets the default image specified in the configuration file /boot/grub2/grub.cfg.

This configuration file is first generated during Linux installation and automatically regenerated whenever a new Linux kernel is installed.

Linux Kernel

In this step, the root filesystem is mounted as specified in the entry *root=* found in the GRUB configuration file. Then the kernel executes the /sbin/init program. The kernel uses a file called *initrd*, short for Initial RAM Disk, as a temporary root filesystem until the kernel is booted and the real root filesystem is mounted. It contains all necessary drivers to access hard drive partitions, filesystems, and other hardware components.

Alternative Boot Loaders

GRUB is not the only boot loader in the open-source world. Other boot loaders include:

BURG

> The name abbreviates to Brand-new Unified Loader from GRUB (a bit of a stretch to get the reverse naming of GRUB if you ask us). It is an offshoot of GRUB with much more room for individual configuration.

SYSLINUX

> A lightweight boot loader for networks and disc drives.

ISOLINUX

> A boot loader from the SYSLINUX project, generally used for Linux Live CDs and bootable install CDs.

gummiboot

> A boot loader for EFI-based computers with a text-mode interface. It is intended to be a minimal alterna-

tive to GNU GRUB that detects bootable images (including Linux kernel images, operating systems, and other boot loaders), does not require a configuration file, provides a basic menu-based interface, and can also integrate with *systemd* to provide performance data.

Libreboot

A lightweight system designed to perform only the minimum number of tasks necessary to load and run a modern 32-bit or 64-bit operating system. The image below shows the menu for Libreboot.

rEFInd

A boot manager for EFI-based computers that features a GUI. rEFInd can be used to boot multiple operating systems, and it also provides a way to enter and explore the EFI pre-boot environment.

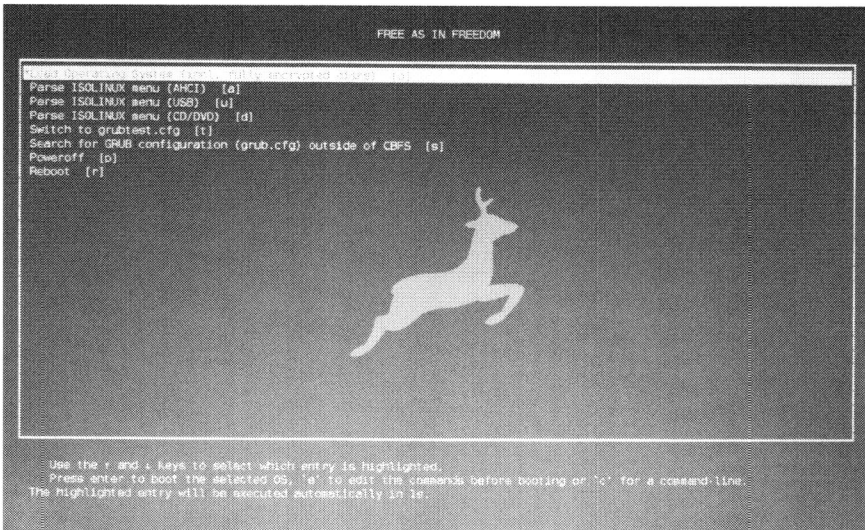

Reviewing the Boot Process

Linux generates a log file to enable a review of the boot process and to read its accompanying messages. Before Linux 8, the boot log was stored as a text file in /var/log/boot. Linux 8 introduced *systemd* and the format and location changed. To retrieve the boot log, use **journalctl** as follows (must be root):

```
# journalctl -b
```

Systemd stores log messages in a special format. **journalctl** reads the log and displays messages in chronological order. The earliest entry comes first and the entries can be scrolled back and forth using the arrow keys. The output consists of four columns: date (timestamp), hostname, message type kernel, and the message itself.

```
...
Aug 20 09:36:08 debian106 kernel: Linux version 4.9.0-7-amd
Aug 20 09:36:08 debian106 kernel: Command line: BOOT_IM
Aug 20 09:36:08 debian106 kernel: x86/fpu: Legacy x87 FPU
Aug 20 09:36:08 debian106 kernel: e820: BIOS-provided phys
Aug 20 09:36:08 debian106 kernel: BIOS-e820: [mem 0x0000
Aug 20 09:36:08 debian106 kernel: BIOS-e820: [mem 0x0000
Aug 20 09:36:08 debian106 kernel: BIOS-e820: [mem 0x0000
Aug 20 09:36:08 debian106 kernel: BIOS-e820: [mem 0x0000
Aug 20 09:36:08 debian106 kernel: BIOS-e820: [mem 0x0000
Aug 20 09:36:08 debian106 kernel: BIOS-e820: [mem 0x0000
Aug 20 09:36:08 debian106 kernel: BIOS-e820: [mem 0x0000
Aug 20 09:36:08 debian106 kernel: NX (Execute Disable prot
Aug 20 09:36:08 debian106 kernel: SMBIOS 2.5 present.
Aug 20 09:36:08 debian106 kernel: DMI: innotek GmbH Virtu
Aug 20 09:36:08 debian106 kernel: e820: update [mem 0x000
...
```

To see the list of recorded boots, the **list-boots** option can be used. The output consists of three columns: the boot entry number (0 for the last entry), a hash to identify the entry, and a timestamp. The example below shows the output.

> \# journalctl --list-boots
> 0 5f41f5e968b34d068320f0f13237b7e2 Tue 2020-09-04 19:16:12 EDT
> lines 1-1/1 (END)

An alternative to **journalctl** is **dmesg**. This command allows you to see the entire boot process, including BIOS messages.

The image above displays the output you would get. Each line consists of three parts: the date (timestamp) printed on the left in brackets, the component printed second and before the colon (:), and the message printed last. On a color monitor, these three parts are distinguished by color i.e. green, yellow, and black.

Stop and Restart Commands

There are several common commands available when it comes to restarting and stopping the system. To reboot Linux, you can use either **reboot** or **shutdown**. To stop Linux, you can invoke **halt**, **poweroff**, or **shutdown**. Next, we will discuss some practical examples.

```
# shutdown -r now
```

The above command will restart the system. The option **-r** designates a reboot and restarts the system. The option **now** is a time parameter and invokes the action immediately. You can also use the **reboot** command to perform the same action as the **shutdown -r now** command.

```
# reboot
```

The **shutdown** command can also be used to stop the system by using the **-h** option instead. This instructs Linux to halt.

```
# shutdown -h now
```

Again, the **now** time parameter is used to stop the system immediately. The time parameter can also be specified as an exact time. The command shown in the following example will shut down the system after five minutes. It will also inform all users about the shutdown by sending them a relevant message. The message will be visible on all open terminals.

```
# shutdown -h +5 "Server shutdown in 5 min"
Shutdown scheduled for Thu 2020-09-06 02:28:30 EDT, use
'shutdown -c' to cancel.
#
```

Similar to rebooting the system, stopping Linux also has a shortcut in the form of the **halt** command. This performs the same action as the **shutdown -h now** command.

```
# halt
```

The **halt**, **poweroff**, and **reboot** commands stop the system immediately. They are similar to **shutdown -h now** except that the **shutdown** command terminates all processes gracefully, instead of killing them abruptly. Keep in mind that all the commands discussed here require administrative privileges to be executed. They cannot be executed by a regular user.

## CHAPTER NINE

Hardware Management

Automatic hardware detection used to be somewhat of a gamble, as hardware wasn't always detected automatically all of the time. It used to be necessary to probe the hardware to figure out what was installed. In the last few years, this has improved significantly as manufacturers document their products in more detail and publish the specs online. This has led to an extended knowledge database and support.

Using the /proc Filesystem

/proc is a virtual filesystem, also referred to as an *in-memory filesystem*, created by the Linux kernel at runtime. It displays information about the kernel, processes, and other system information. This information is displayed in a file structure and accessible to everyone.

```
$ cat /proc/cmdline
BOOT_IMAGE=/boot/vmlinux-4.9.0-7-amd64 root=UUID
=1d4acbbf-4420-4eab-984d-ceebc408a51e ro quiet
$
```

As an example, the command on the previous page shows the contents of /proc/cmdline, which are the options the Linux kernel was invoked with. Recall that **cat** outputs the contents of a file to the screen. Some other useful files are:

/proc/cpuinfo

Information about the computer's CPU.

/proc/meminfo

Information about system memory.

/proc/loadvg

Load average. The first three columns measure CPU utilization from the last 1, 5, and 10 minutes. The fourth column shows the number of currently running processes and the total number of processes. The last column displays the last process ID used.

/proc/partitions

Partition-related information.

/proc/version

Information about the Linux version.

```
$ cat /proc/version
Linux version 3.16.0-4-amd64 (debian-
kernel@lists.debian.org) (gcc version 4.8.4 (Debian 4.8.4-1) )
#1 SMP Debian 3.16.43-2+deb8u2 (2017-06-26)
$
```

/proc/filesystems

Lists the filesystems supported by the kernel.

/proc/devices

List of device drivers configured into the currently running kernel.

/proc/uptime

Contains information about the running time of the system. The first number is the total number of seconds the system has been up. The second number is how much of that time the machine has spent idle, in seconds.

```
$ cat /proc/uptime
15250.54 55603.02
$
```

Processes in Linux are assigned several files. The example below shows the file structure for the process with the Process ID (PID) of 433. Following this, we look at the purpose and contents of the files generally available.

```
|- 433
|    |- attr
|    |- cwd -> /home/user
|    |- fd
|    |- fdinfo
|    |- map_files
|    |- net
|    |   |- dev_snmp6
|    |   |- netfilter
|    |   |- stat
|    |- ns
|    |- root -> /
|    |- task
```

Process Files

File Path	Description
/proc/PID/cmdline	Command line arguments
/proc/PID/cpu	Current and last CPU in which the process was executed
/proc/PID/cwd	Link to the current working directory
/proc/PID/environ	Values of the environment variables
/proc/PID/exe	Link to the executable of this process
/proc/PID/fd	Directory that contains all file descriptors
/proc/PID/maps	Maps to executables and library files
/proc/PID/mem	Memory held by this process
/proc/PID/root	Link to the root directory of this process
/proc/PID/stat	Status of the process
/proc/PID/statm	Process memory status information
/proc/PID/status	Process status in human readable form

If you want to learn more about the /proc filesystem, check out the Man Page (short for Manual Pages) for /proc. It covers much more than what is relevant for the scope of this guide. Access to Man Pages is discussed in Chapter 19.

Command Line Tools

Detect CPU Using cpuid

In order to get more information about the CPU in your Linux system, use the **cpuid** command. This tool is available from the Debian package named *cpuid*. An example of the detailed information returned by this command is shown below.

```
$ cpuid CPU 0:
vendor_id = "GenuineIntel"
version information (1/eax):
processor type          = primary processor (0)
family                  = Intel Pentium Pro/II/III
                          /Celeron/Core/Core 2/Atom,
                          AMD Athlon/Duron -, Cyrix M2,
                          VIA C3 (6)
model                   = 0xd (13)
stepping id             = 0x4 (4)
extended family         = 0x0 (0)
extended model          = 0x3 (3)
(simple synth)          = Intel Pentium II / Pentium III /
                          Pentium M / Celeron / Celeron M
                          / - Core / Core 2 / Core i / Xeon /
                          Atom (unknown model)
miscellaneous (1/ebx):
process local APIC physical ID    = 0x0 (0)
cpu count                         = 0x10 (16)
CLFLUSH line size                 = 0x8 (8)
brand index                       = 0x0 (0)
brand id                          = 0x00 (0): unknown
feature information (1/edx):
x87 FPU on chip                       = true
virtual-8086 mode enhancement         = true
...
$
```

Detect Hardware Using dmidecode

The command **dmidecode** reports detailed data about installed system components such as the processor, motherboard, and RAM. This information is based on the Desktop Management Interface (DMI), which is a framework that classifies the individual components of a desktop, notebook, or server by abstracting them from the software that manages them. This tool is available via the Debian package of the same name. The example below shows the output when executed in Debian via a VirtualBox environment.

```
# dmidecode
# dmidecode 3.0
Getting SMBIOS data from sysfs.
SMBIOS 2.5 present.
10 structures occupying 450 bytes.
Table at 0x000E1000.

Handle 0x0000, DMI type 0, 20 bytes
BIOS Information
      Vendor: innotek GmbH
      Version: VirtualBox
      Release Date: 12/01/2006
      Address: 0xE0000
      Runtime Size: 128 kB
      Characteristics:
            ISA is supported
            PCI is supported
            Boot from CD is supported
            Selectable boot is supported
            8042 keyboard services are supported (int 9h)
            CGA/mono video services are supported (int 10h
            ACPI is supported
Handle 0x0001, DMI type 1, 27 bytes
...
```

Graphical Tools

Graphical tools are also available that can collect and display hardware information. These tools provide a graphical user interface, which many users prefer. Some of these tools include Hardware Lister (lshw-gtk) and the Debian package *hardinfo*. The image below presents memory information using *hardinfo*.

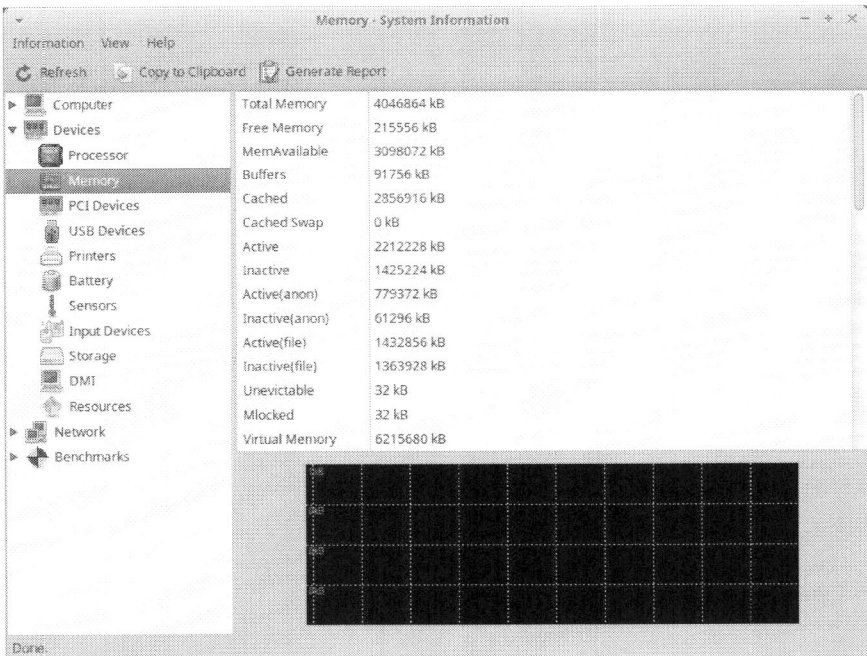

## CHAPTER TEN

User and Group Management

Linux is a multi-user operating system, which means multiple users can have access to the system at the same time. For the system to manage these different users and groups, it stores this data in several configuration files:

/etc/passwd	User data.
/etc/shadow	Encrypted user passwords.
/etc/group	Group data.
/etc/gshadow	Encrypted group passwords.

These files are text-based databases and have a defined structure. Below we will look at each in more detail. The contents of these files can be changed using a text editor, or with the commands **passwd**, **chage**, **chfn**, **usermod**, and **chsh**.

/etc/passwd

This file contains all user attributes except the password. Each line consists of seven columns, and the columns are separated by a colon (:). The attributes are the username, the password, the user ID, the group ID, the GECOS field, the user's home directory, and the user's login shell.

The first attribute *username* refers to the UNIX username and it must be unique to the system. The *password* field only contains an x. The value of the password itself has moved to /etc/shadow (see next section) and the attribute is only kept for backward compatibility. *UID* refers to the User ID, and the range of the unique numeric value can be between 0 and 65535. On Debian, the root user has a UID of 0, services then range from 1 to 999, and regular users start at 1000. The example below shows the info for a root user and a regular user.

```
$ grep root /etc/passwd
root:x:0:0:root:/root:/bin/bash
$ grep user /etc/passwd
user:x:1000:1000:Debian Us-
er,123,456,135:/home/user:/bin/bash
$
```

The *GID* attribute refers to the Group ID for the user's primary group. *GECOS* is short for General Comprehensive Operating System and contains the user's full name and sometimes a comma-separated list of user data like room and telephone number. *Home* is the user's home directory and *shell* is the default shell for the user. To be precise, it is the program that is executed as soon as the user logs in.

/etc/shadow

This file contains the encrypted passwords and expiration data of users. The format is similar to /etc/passwd which we discussed above. Each line consists of eight columns, and the columns are separated by a colon. The attributes are the username, the password, the date of the last change, the minimum usage value, the maximum usage value, the warning time, the inactivity period, and the expiration date.

The first attribute *username* again refers to the UNIX username, but in this instance, the *password* field does contain the user's encrypted password. *lastchange* indicates the days since 1/1/1970 that the password was last changed. The next two attributes *minimum* and *maximum* show the minimum number of days before the user can change their password, and the maximum number of days the password is still valid. *Warn* shows the number of days before the password expiring, that the user will be warned to change the password.

The *inactive* attribute is the number of days after expiration until the user is disabled, and the *expiration date* is the number of days after 1/1/1970 since the account has been disabled. The example below shows the attributes for a regular user. The password is stored as a salted hash value in the second column.

```
# grep user /etc/shadow
user:$6$QB0brhON$R9saRX5Q1/OwYWyw4SViqeh6Mcu...
CshFyblLBTZxlCoggH12p21:17763:0:99999:7:::
```

To show the account details, invoke the **chage** command followed by the option -l (short for --list) along with the username. The example below lists the details for the user named *user*.

```
# chage -l user
Last password change        : Aug 20, 2020
Password expires            : never
Password inactive           : never
Account expires             : never
Minimum number of days between password change : 0
Maximum number of days between password change : 99999
Number of days of warning before password expires  : 7
#
```

As you can see from this example, the account does not have an expiration date. In order to set this value to 31 December 2019, invoke the **usermod** command with the option **-e** (short for --expiredate) along with the username.

```
# usermod -e 2019-12-31 user
```

To lock and unlock the user account the **usermod** command has two options **-L** (short for --lock) and **-U** (short for --unlock). The next example locks the account for the user named *user*. The user can still work and finish his session but is not able to log into the system anymore.

```
# usermod -L user
```

/etc/group

This file contains the user group attributes. Each line consists of four columns, and the columns are separated once again by a colon. The attributes are the group name, the password, the group ID, and the list of its members. The *groupname* attribute is similar to the username attribute and refers to the UNIX group name, which must be a unique name on the system. The *password* field contains an x because the value has been moved to the file /etc/gshadow, and the field is kept only for backward compatibility.

The *members* attribute provides a comma-separated list of users with access to the group. *GID* is the unique Group ID, which has a numeric range between 0 and 65535, with a similar allocation as we have with the UID. The user root has a GID of 0, services will range from 1 to 999, and regular users start at 1000. The following code snippet shows this for the root and a regular user.

```
$ grep root /etc/group
root:x:0:
$ egrep "^user" /etc/group
user:x:1000:
$
```

The example below shows the name of the groups which the user named *user* is part of.

```
$ grep user /etc/group
cdrom:x:24:user
floppy:x:25:user
audio:x:29:user,pulse
dip:x:30:user
video:x:44:user
plugdev:x:46:user
users:x:100:
netdev:x:108:user
bluetooth:x:111:user
user:x:1000:
$
```

/etc/gshadow

This file contains the encrypted passwords and user data for groups. The format is similar to /etc/shadow. Each line consists of four columns separated by a colon. The attributes are the group name, the password, the administrators, and the list of members.

The *groupname* attribute is again the UNIX group name, with the *password* being the encrypted password. *Administrators* are group members who can add or remove other members using the **gpasswd** command, and *members* are non-administrative members of the group.

User and Group Commands

There are several commands available to manage users and groups in a Linux system. We will look at commands needed to view and change user information, change passwords, create and delete user accounts, as well as look into group commands. Unless stated otherwise, these commands can be run as a regular user.

whoami

This command returns your current user ID as follows:

```
$ whoami
user
$
```

users, who and w

The **who** command shows the users that are currently logged into your Linux system. The output's first column starts with the login name of the user. This is followed by the name of the terminal, where *console* represents a login terminal and *pts* abbreviates a pseudo-terminal session. The last two columns contain the login time and the host the user comes from in brackets.

```
$ who
user        console      2020-08-20 09:36 (:0)
user        pts/2        2020-08-20 09:47 (:0)
user        pts/3        2020-08-20 09:47 (:0)
$
```

w extends the output of **who** by adding additional information. The single columns for **w** contain the login name of the user (LOGIN), the name of the terminal (TTY), the name of the host the user comes from (FROM), the login time (LOG-IN@), the idle time (IDLE), the CPU usage (JCPU and PCPU) as well as the last command the user executed (WHAT).

```
$ w
 09:49:23 up 9 min,  3 users,  load average: 0.15, 0.03, 0.01
 USER  TTY      FROM LOGIN@ IDLE JCPU  PCPU  WHAT
 user  console :0       09:36    13:14 0.00s 0.04s  :0
 user  pts/2   :0       09:47    2:03  0.02s 0.02s  xterm
 user  pts/3   :0       09:47    2:03  0.01s 0.01s  bash
 $
```

In contrast to the above, **users** simply outputs the name of the users as a space-separated list in a single line.

```
$ users
user user user
$
```

id and groups

The **id** command outputs the user and group information of the current user (see below). From left to right the columns show the user ID (UID), the group ID (GID), and the name of the groups the user is a member of.

```
$ id
uid=1000(user) gid=1000(user) groups=1000(user),
24(cdrom), 25(floppy), 29(audio), 30(dip), 44(video),
46(plugdev), 108(netdev), 111(bluetooth)
$
```

To list the names of all the groups the user belongs to, you can also invoke the **groups** command. The output is a space-separated list of the group names.

```
$ groups
user cdrom floppy audio dip video plugdev netdev bluetooth
$
```

passwd

As described in Chapter 4, the Linux system has at least two users: an administrative root user and a regular user that we simply called *user*. Every account is also secured with a password.

In order to change your password, use the **passwd** command from the Debian *passwd* package. As shown below, type in the current password first, press Enter, type in the new password, press Enter to confirm, retype the new password and press Enter to confirm again.

```
$ passwd
Changing password for user.
(current) UNIX password:
Enter new UNIX password:
Retype new UNIX password:
passwd: password updated successfully
$
```

As a regular user, you are allowed to change your own password only. The administrative root user can set a new password for itself and other users as well. In such a scenario, we call **passwd** by adding the user name.

```
# passwd felix
Changing password for felix.
(current) UNIX password:
Enter new UNIX password:
Retype new UNIX password:
passwd: password updated successfully
#
```

The password is stored as a hashed value in the configuration file named /etc/shadow. The content of this file is only visible to the administrative user. The example below shows how to extract the information for the user *user* with the help of the **grep** command.

```
# grep user /etc/shadow
user:$6$QB0brhON$R9saRX5Q1/OwYWyw4SViqeh6Mcu ...
CshFyblLBTZxlCoggH12p21:17763:0:99999:7:::
#
```

chfn

This command is also from the Debian *passwd* package and changes the user information that is stored on your system in /etc/passwd. The basic setup was already done during the installation of your Debian system. To modify this information, you can run **chfn** without further parameters in interactive mode, or with one or more of the following options to adapt only a specific value:

-f   For --full-name. Changes the full name of the user.

-h   For --home-phone. Changes the home phone number.

-r   For --room. Changes the room number of the user.

-w   For --work-phone. Changes the work phone number.

The following example changes the entry for the home phone number to 135:

```
$ chfn -h 135
Password:
$
```

chsh

This command (also from the Debian *passwd* package) changes the entry for the shell that you use to log into your Linux system. Again, this information is stored in /etc/passwd. Which shells are allowed to be used are limited by the entries in the configuration file named /etc/shells. **chsh** works similar to the **chfn** command. Invoked without further options, an interactive method is used:

```
$ chsh
Password:
Changing the login shell for user
Enter the new value, or press ENTER for the default
        Login Shell [/bin/sh]: /bin/bash
$
```

chsh accepts the option -s (short for --shell) to set the shell in non-interactive mode. The following example shows the command line call:

```
$ chsh -s /bin/bash
$
```

In order to modify the shell for a different user other than yourself, invoke the **chsh** command with the user's name as a parameter. Note that only the administrative user can do this for another user. The next example shows how to do that for the user *felix*.

```
# chsh felix
Changing the login shell for felix
Enter the new value, or press ENTER for the new value
          Login shell [/bin/bash]:
#
```

su and sudo

To change your role from one user to another, you can utilize the **su** command. **su** abbreviates *switch user*. Invoked without further options, you change to the root user as follows:

```
$ su
Password:
#
```

Working as the administrative root user comes with great responsibility and presumes that you know exactly what you are doing. To work as a different user than root, invoke the **su** command with the desired user's name as follows:

```
$ su felix
Password:
$
```

The **su** command changes the current role permanently. In order to run only a single command as an administrative user, use the **sudo** command. This requires the Debian **sudo** package to be installed and the additional user to be added to the configuration file /etc/sudoers using the **visudo** command.

adduser

The command **adduser** creates new user accounts. The example below shows the information that is required. This includes a new entry in the file /etc/passwd as well as the creation of a new group, plus home directory. Furthermore, prepared data from the directory /etc/skel is copied into the previously created home directory. Afterward, the account information is modified using the **chsh** command.

```
# adduser caro
Adding user 'caro' ...
Adding new group 'caro' (1002) ...
Adding new user 'caro' (1002) with group 'caro' ...
Creating home directory '/home/caro' ...
Copying files from '/etc/skel' ...
Enter new UNIX password:
Retype new UNIX password:
passwd: password updated successfully
Changing the user information for caro
Enter the new value, or press ENTER for the default
        Full Name []: Caro
        Room Number []:
        Work Phone []:
        Home Phone []:
        Other []:
Is the information correct? [Y/n] y
#
```

Having set up the new user, the entry in /etc/passwd looks as follows:

```
# grep caro /etc/passwd
caro:x:1002:1002:Caro, , , :/home/caro:/bin/bash
#
```

deluser

Deleting user accounts is done with the help of the **deluser** command while deleting a group can be done via **delgroup**. To delete a user without deleting any of the user's files, use the following command as the root user:

```
# deluser felix
```

The **deluser** command has the following options available to fine-tune its execution:

--group	Delete a group, same as **delgroup**.
--system	Delete a user only if it is a system user.
--backup	Backup the user's files contained in the home directory to a file named /$user.tar.gz or /$user.tar.bz2.
--backup-to	Backup the user's files contained in the home directory to a specified file.
--remove-all-files	Remove all files from the system that are owned by the user. If a backup is specified, the files will be deleted after performing the backup.

```
# deluser --remove-all-files felix
```

## CHAPTER ELEVEN

Filesystems

A filesystem is a way of controlling how data is stored on a drive. If data was not structured, there would be no way of knowing where a particular entry ends and the next one begins. Filesystems separate the data into pieces and each piece has a unique name. This way, information is easily isolated and identified. Each group of data on a filesystem is called an entry. Entries in a filesystem can be files, directories (also named folders), references (also named links), sockets, and fifos (also known as named pipes). Each entry in the filesystem contains the following data about it:

name

> The name of the entry.

permissions

> Which user is the owner of the entry and is allowed to read, write, and execute the entry.

creation time, last modified time, last access time

> The time the entry was created, modified, or accessed last.

file size, number of blocks, IO blocks

How much disk space does the entry need in the filesystem.

inode number

Short for index node and refers to the block number where the data entry starts.

number of symlinks

Number of references or symbolic links that point to that entry.

You can retrieve the above information by using the **stat** command. **stat** is part of the Debian package *coreutils* and only requires the name of an entry to be examined. The example below displays the information for the file *documentation.pdf*.

```
$ stat documentation.pdf
File:       documentation.pdf
Size:       512           Blocks: 8        IO Block: 4096 reg
Device:     808h/2056d    Inode: 260927 Links: 1
Access:     (0644/-rw-r--r--)   Uid: (0/root)   Gid: (0/root)
Access:     2020-09-04 18:44:30.071901792 -0400
Modify:     2020-09-04 18:44:22.358157773 -0400
Change:     2020-09-06 18:08:14.528658813 -0400
Birth:      -
$
```

This information can also be viewed in a slightly more re-fined way with Midnight Commander (mc), or with a right-click on a file icon that resides on the XFCE desktop. Both options are shown on the adjacent page.

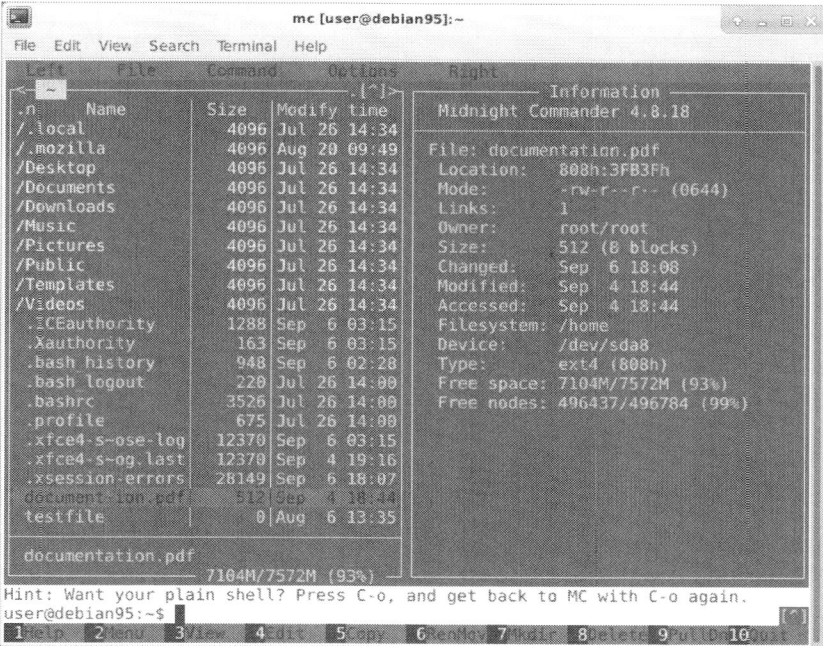

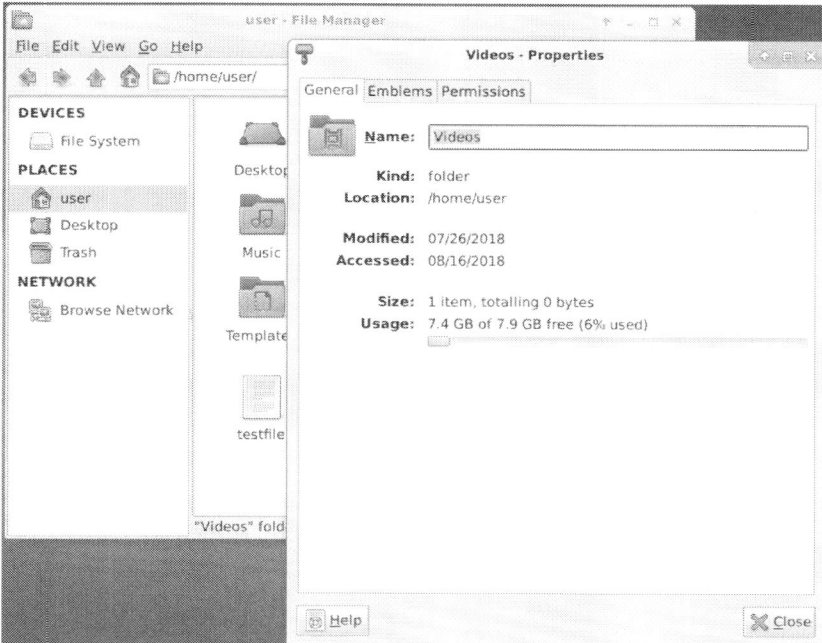

Types of Commonly Used Filesystems

A number of filesystems are quite popular and widely used. This includes FAT, ext2, ext3, ext4, JFS, XFS, ZFS, ReiserFS, and SWAP. Let's look at each of these in more detail.

File Allocation Table (FAT)

FAT was introduced in 1977 for floppy disks and then used for hard disks through the DOS and Microsoft Windows 9X era. It is supported by nearly all operating systems to date and is useful as a data transfer medium between different systems. It is commonly used on external media such as USB drives. The original FAT system was only an 8-bit system with a maximum file size of 8MB, supporting 6:3 filenames and no subdirectories. There are 3 main variants of FAT:

FAT12

12-bit File Allocation Table. Supports maximum volume sizes of 16MB with 4KB clusters or 32MB with 8KB clusters.

FAT16

16-bit File Allocation Table. Supports maximum volume sizes of 2GB with 32KB clusters or 4GB with 64KB clusters. Filenames must be in the 8:3 format with OEM characters or 256 UCS characters.

FAT32

Supports a maximum file size of 2TB with 512B sectors, 8TB with 2KB sectors and 32K clusters, or 16TB with 4KB sectors and 64K clusters. Filenames must be in the 8:3 format with OEM characters or 256 UCS characters.

Second Extended File System (ext2)

This was the first consumer-grade filesystem for Linux and was the default filesystem for Linux distributions such as RedHat and Debian until ext3 became mainstream in 2001. Today, it is still in use on storage devices like digital memory cards, where the journaling functionality of ext3 or ext4 is not needed. This increases performance and minimizes the number of writes.

Third Extended File System (ext3)

Ext3 is a journaled version of ext2 and can be upgraded directly from ext2 without the need for backup and restore operations. Ext3 is not as fast as ext4, JFS, XFS, or ReiserFS but it uses less CPU power than ReiserFS or XFS. Ext3 supports files up to 16GB and filesystems up to 32TiB in size.

Fourth Extended File System (ext4)

Ext4 is an extension of ext3 with extra features such as large filesystem support. It supports files up to 16TiB and filesystems up to 1EiB in size. Furthermore, it features *extents*. An *extent* is a contiguous range of blocks which makes handling very large files more efficient.

Journaled File System (JFS)

JFS was originally developed for IBM's AIX Unix operating system and later ported to OS/2. JFS is a fully 64bit filesystem that uses extents, supports unlimited small files, and large files up to 4 PB. It is ideal for extremely large filesystems.

XFS

XFS is a journaling filesystem developed by Silicon Graphics (SGI) in 1993 for the IRIX operating system. It subdivides physical volumes into allocations allowing more efficient parallel I/O and filesystem bandwidth, and supports large files up to 8EiB.

ZFS

The Zettabyte File System (ZFS) combines a filesystem and a logical volume manager (LVM). Released by SUN Microsystems in 2005, it is scalable and includes extensive protection against data corruption, support for high storage capacities, efficient data compression, integration of filesystem and volume management, snapshots and copy-on-write clones, continuous integrity checking and automatic repair, RAID-Z, and native Access Control Lists (ACLs) for the Network File System (NFS) version 4. The two projects *OpenZFS* and *ZFS on Linux* continue the development of this filesystem.

ReiserFS

ReiserFS is a general-purpose journaled filesystem that uses the Apple Partition Map based on B+Trees for managing directory contents. ReiserFS version 3 was the default filesystem used in SUSE, Elive, Xandros, Linspire, and YOPER distributions. Support for ReiserFS version 4 has declined to the point where development has halted, other than being made compatible with newer Linux kernels.

Swap Space

Swap space is used by Linux to swap out pages of memory when they are not in use. Swap space is not accessible to the user and cannot be used for normal file storage. The space used by swap space is as follows:

Desktop systems

Use 2x the total amount of memory on the system. That way if many large programs are running concurrently, the unused memory can be saved to disk and programs run more efficiently.

Server systems

Use 0.5x the total amount of memory. Servers should not be doing a lot of swapping, so half the total memory is enough.

Old systems

Systems with memory less than 1GB. Use as much swap space as possible, as the system will need to do a lot of swapping to run efficiently.

Instead of a separate swap partition, it is also possible to use a swap file. This is created using **dd** to create a fixed size file on an existing partition. This has the advantages of not requiring a fixed swap partition and it can be resized later for efficiency.

Filesystem Commands

The following commands are used to manage filesystems:

mkfs	Abbreviation for *make file system* and creates a filesystem.
mkswap	Abbreviation for *make swap* and creates a swap filesystem.
badblocks	Shows bad blocks on a filesystem.
fsck	Abbreviation for *file system check* and examines and repairs a Linux filesystem.
dumpe2fs	Shows information about a filesystem.
file	Determines the type of entry in the filesystem.

link and unlink	Creates and deletes links to a file.
ln	Abbreviation for *link* and creates hard links and soft links.
ls	Displays information about an entry (file, directory, link, socket, or fifo).
lsof	Shows the list of opened files.
stat	Shows all the information that is kept for an entry.
fdisk and cfdisk	Show, create, and delete partitions with filesystems on a drive. The image below shows a screen of **cfdisk**.

```
                            user@debian95: ~
 File   Edit   View   Search   Terminal   Help
                            Disk: /dev/sda
                 Size: 15 GiB, 16106127360 bytes, 31457280 sectors
                        Label: dos, identifier: 0x1c248227

      Device       Boot       Start        End   Sectors   Size Id Type
      /dev/sda1      *          2048    5896191   5894144   2.8G 83 Linux
      /dev/sda2               5898238   31455231  25556994  12.2G  5 Extended
 >>   ├─/dev/sda5            5898240    8511487   2613248   1.3G 83 Linux
      ├─/dev/sda6            8513536   14954495   6440960   3.1G 82 Linux swap / Solaris
      ├─/dev/sda7           14956544   15564799    608256   297M 83 Linux
      └─/dev/sda8           15566848   31455231  15888384   7.6G 83 Linux




   Partition type: Linux (83)
 Filesystem UUID: e2fd3efb-59d2-4f2a-9841-5febe7ca2e6a
       Filesystem: ext4
       Mountpoint: /var (mounted)

   [Bootable]  [ Delete ]  [  Quit  ]  [ Type  ]  [ Help  ]  [ Write ]
   [ Dump  ]

                   Quit program without writing changes
```

sync	Syncing the drive cache with the disk.
mount and umount	Enabling or disabling a device with a filesystem.
tune2fs	Adjusts filesystem parameters on ext2, ext3, and ext4 filesystems.

Practical Example

In the following example, we will look at how to use the commands we discussed above. We will emulate a memory disk, create a proper filesystem on it, mount it, and store data on it. To start, we will create a file with a size of 10MB using **dd** as follows:

```
$ dd if=/dev/zero of=memory.image bs=512b count=40
```

The file consists of zeroes only, as the data is read from a device named /dev/zero that returns zeroes only (if= /dev/zero). The output is written to the file *memory.image* with a block size of 512 bytes forty times. The example below shows the output of **dd** and the size of the output file using **ls**.

```
$ dd if=/dev/zero of=memory.image bs=512b count=40
40+0 records in
40+0 records out
10485760 bytes (10 MB, 10MiB) copied, 0.01563 s, 671 MB/s
$ ls -lah memory.image
-rw-r--r-- 1 user user 10M Sep 9 05:28 memory.image
$
```

For the next step, we create an ext4 filesystem on the file using the command **mkfs.ext4**:

```
$ /sbin/mkfs.ext4 memory.image 10M
mke2fs 1.43.4 (31-Jan-2017)
Discarding device blocks: done
Creating filesystem with 10240 1k blocks and 2560 inodes
Filesystem UUID: 52c89176-a665-48b3-9bf6-2abb9b2ad721
Superblock backups stored on blocks:
        8193

Allocating group tables: done
Writing inode tables: done
Creating journal (1024 blocks): done
Writing superblocks and filesystem accounting information:
done

$ ls -lah memory.image
-rw-r--r-- 1 user user 10M Sep 9 05:40 memory.image
$
```

This results in a filesystem with 10240 blocks of 1K with space for 2560 entries. Next, we create a mount point using the **mkdir** command:

```
$ mkdir /tmp/image
```

The mount command helps to integrate the image as follows:

```
$ su
Password:
# mount memory.image /tmp/image
#
```

Now we can store data on the mounted device. Here, the command **cp** comes into play. The **cp** command copies files. To operate properly, it requires two names: the name of the original file and the name of the copy.

The original file is not touched and stays intact. The copy has the same contents as the original, but with the current timestamp. Use the option **-i** (or --interactive) to prevent overwriting existing files. In the example below, we use **cp -v** to produce additional output.

```
$ su
Password:
# cp -v documentation.pdf /tmp/image/.
'documentation.pdf' -> '/tmp/image/./documentation.pdf'
# ls /tmp/image/
documentation.pdf lost+found
# sync
# umount /tmp/image
#
```

Before unmounting the device, issue **sync** to clear the cache and write the data to disk. Finally, we can unmount the filesystem as follows:

```
# umount /tmp/image
# exit
$
```

## CHAPTER TWELVE

Disk Storage Management

In this chapter we will look at how to deal with storage devices and filesystems, this includes naming the devices, partition types and schemes, as well as mounting and unmounting partitions.

Naming the Devices

Everything in Linux is a file, a directory is a file and a device is a file too. Every drive on the system is represented as a block device inside the /dev folder. When the system starts up, the *udev* service is run, which detects all devices in /dev and then mounts them accordingly. Inside /dev, IDE drives have the names *hda*, *hdb* all the way up to *hdp*. Other device types such as SCSI, USB, SATA, and PATA are represented as *sda*, *sdb* up to *sdp*. Drives such as CD or DVD drives receive labels like *cdrom* or *dvd* whereas it is common that SD cards are labeled with *mmcblk*.

Each drive must have at least one partition if it is to run on the system. A drive can have up to 16 partitions, each with its own filesystem. Within each device, partitions are then labeled *sda1*, *sda2* up to *sda16* for the device /dev/sda. Linux has a limit of sixteen drives with sixteen partitions each.

Primary, Extended, and Logical Partitions

Each drive can have up to four primary partitions, or three primary partitions and one extended partition. Furthermore, an extended partition can contain up to sixteen logical partitions. If a system contains only four primary partitions, they are numbered sda1 through sda4 as follows:

```
/dev/sda1
/dev/sda2
/dev/sda3
/dev/sda4
```

If a system contains three primary partitions and one extended partition, which contains logical partitions, primary partition sda4 falls away and is replaced with logical partitions sda5, sda6, sda7 etc:

```
/dev/sda1
/dev/sda2
/dev/sda3
/dev/sda5
/dev/sda6
/dev/sda7
```

The first logical partition is always numbered as *sda5*. So even if there are less than three primary partitions, they are numbered as follows:

```
/dev/sda1
/dev/sda5
/dev/sda6
```

To see the partition structure, the command **lsblk** from the *util-linux* package is quite helpful. **lsblk** abbreviates the term *list block devices*. The command can output all the block devices that are in use (see example below). The seven columns represent the following information:

NAME   The name of the device.

MAJ:MIN   The major number and minor number of the device.

RM   0 if the device is fixed and 1 if the device can be removed.

SIZE   The size of the device in a human-readable format.

RO   1 if the device is read-only and 0 if not.

TYPE   The type of device. Loop represents a loop device, disk a hard disk, part refers to a partition of a disk, lvm is a partition run by a Logical Volume Manager (LVM), and rom refers to a CD/DVD rom.

MOUNTPOINT   Lists the directory the device is mounted to.

```
$ lsblk
NAME    MAJ:MIN  RM   SIZE    RO   TYPE    MOUNTP
sda     8:0      0    15G     0    disk
|-sda1  8:1      0    2.8G    0    part    /
```

|—sda2	8:2	0	1K	0	part	
|—sda5	8:5	0	1.3G	0	part	/var
|—sda6	8:6	0	3.1G	0	part	[SWAP]
|—sda7	8:7	0	297M	0	part	/tmp
|—sda8	8:8	0	7.6G	0	part	/home
sr0	11:0	1	1024M	0	rom	

The **lsblk** command can also output all the unused devices:

```
$ lsblk -a
```

NAME	MAJ:MIN	RM	SIZE	RO	TYPE	MOUNTP
loop0	7:0	0		0	loop	
loop1	7:1	0		0	loop	
loop2	7:2	0		0	loop	
loop3	7:3	0		0	loop	
loop4	7:4	0		0	loop	
loop5	7:5	0		0	loop	
loop6	7:6	0		0	loop	
loop7	7:7	0		0	loop	
sda	8:0	0	15G	0	disk	
|—sda1	8:1	0	2.8G	0	part	/
|—sda2	8:2	0	1K	0	part	
|—sda5	8:5	0	1.3G	0	part	/var
|—sda6	8:6	0	3.1G	0	part	[SWAP]
|—sda7	8:7	0	297M	0	part	/tmp
|—sda8	8:8	0	7.6G	0	part	/home
sr0	11:0	1	1024M	0	rom	

```
$
```

To list the mounted filesystems, use either the **mount** command or the **findmnt** command. Both commands are part of the *mount* package. Invoked without further options, **findmnt** prints all the mounted filesystems. This list can be quite long. In order to only select the ext4 filesystems the option -t **ext4** (short for --type ext4) is can be used (see example blow). The four output columns contain the following information:

TARGET	The mount point, which is the directory the device is mounted to in the system.
SOURCE	The device name.
FSTYPE	The filesystem type.
OPTIONS	The options which were used to mount the device.

```
$ findmnt -t ext4
TARGET   SOURCE      FSTYPE   OPTIONS
/        /dev/sda1   ext4     rw,relatime,errors=remou
|-/home  /dev/sda8   ext4     rw,relatime,data=ordered
|-/tmp   /dev/sda7   ext4     rw,relatime,data=ordered
|-/var   /dev/sda5   ext4     rw,relatime,data=ordered
$
```

udev, df and du

udev is an abbreviation of *userspace /dev* and is a device manager for the Linux kernel. Once *udev* runs, the drives it found are shown in the /dev/disk directory. This contains several subdirectories with symbolic links as listed below.

Note that the number of subdirectories is specific to the Linux release and depends on the version of the Linux kernel. Whenever a disk is recognized by the Linux system, the information is shown here. We can use this information to find which mount points are in use.

/dev/disk/by-id

This shows the partition names that Linux sees and which mount points point to them.

```
# ls -al /dev/disk/by-id
total 0
drwxr-xr-x 2 root root 220 Sep 5 07:14 .
drwxr-xr-x 7 root root 140 Sep 5 07:14 ..
lrwxrwxrwx 1 root ... ata-VBOX_CD-ROM_VBO-01f00.../sr0
lrwxrwxrwx 1 root ... ata-VBOX_HARDDISK_VBb9372.../sda
lrwxrwxrwx 1 root ... ata-VBOX_HARDDISK...part1.../sda1
lrwxrwxrwx 1 root ... ata-VBOX_HARDDISK...part2.../sda2
lrwxrwxrwx 1 root ... ata-VBOX_HARDDISK...part3.../sda3
lrwxrwxrwx 1 root ... ata-VBOX_HARDDISK...part5.../sda5
lrwxrwxrwx 1 root ... ata-VBOX_HARDDISK...part6.../sda6
lrwxrwxrwx 1 root ... ata-VBOX_HARDDISK...part7.../sda7
lrwxrwxrwx 1 root ... ata-VBOX_HARDDISK_VBc544.../sdb
```

/dev/disk/by-path

This shows lower-level hardware definitions and which mount points mount to them.

```
# ls -al /dev/disk/by-path
total 0
drwxr-xr-x 2 root root 220 Sep 5 07:14 .
drwxr-xr-x 7 root root 140 Sep 5 07:14 ..
lrwxrwxrwx 1 root root ... pci-0000:00:01.1-ata-1.../sr0
lrwxrwxrwx 1 root root ... pci-0000:00:0d.0-ata-1.../sda
lrwxrwxrwx 1 root root ... pci-0000:00:0d.0...part1.../sda1
lrwxrwxrwx 1 root root ... pci-0000:00:0d.0...part2.../sda2
lrwxrwxrwx 1 root root ... pci-0000:00:0d.0...part3.../sda3
lrwxrwxrwx 1 root root ... pci-0000:00:0d.0...part5.../sda5
lrwxrwxrwx 1 root root ... pci-0000:00:0d.0...part6.../sda6
lrwxrwxrwx 1 root root ... pci-0000:00:0d.0...part7.../sda7
lrwxrwxrwx 1 root root ... pci-0000:00:0d.0-ata-2.../sdb
```

/dev/disk/by-label

This shows which labels are applied to which mount points.

```
# ls -al /dev/disk/by-label
total 0
drwxr-xr-x 2 root root 220 Sep 5 07:14 .
drwxr-xr-x 7 root root 140 Sep 5 07:14 ..
lrwxrwxrwx 1 root root 10 Sep 5 07:14 home -> ../../sda7
lrwxrwxrwx 1 root root 10 Sep 5 07:14 root -> ../../sda1
lrwxrwxrwx 1 root root 10 Sep 5 07:14 tmp -> ../../sda5
lrwxrwxrwx 1 root root 10 Sep 5 07:14 var -> ../../sda6
```

/dev/disk/by-uuid

This shows the UUID labels for each mount point.

```
# ls -al /dev/disk/by-uuid
total 0
drwxr-xr-x 2 root root 140 Sep 5 07:14 .
drwxr-xr-x 7 root root 140 Sep 5 07:14 ..
lrwxrwxrwx 1 root root ... 9ef7106a-c885-4cbe-aaa1.../sda2
lrwxrwxrwx 1 root root ... ac2823cc-a7b4-4bf3-808e.../sda7
lrwxrwxrwx 1 root root ... d2f4fd43-4f76-414c-9afa.../sda6
lrwxrwxrwx 1 root root ... dc78e6f6-8a4f-4be0-9192.../sda1
lrwxrwxrwx 1 root root ... faef6770-b865-43d2-b1f6.../sda5
```

/dev/disk/by-partuuid

This a component of GUID Partition Tables (GPT) which is a replacement for Master Boot Record (MBR) related disk partitioning.

df and du

To see which filesystems are mounted, and how many blocks are used and available, invoke the **df** command. **df** is an abbreviation for *disk free*. The command offers various options:

df	List in default block size. Sometimes this uses 500KB which can be confusing.
df -h	List in a human-readable format.
df -k	List in kilobytes.
df -m	List in megabytes.

```
# df -k
Filesystem   1K-blocks   Used      Available   Use%  Mounted
udev         1015136     0         1015136     0%    /dev
tmpfs        205256      2984      202272      2%    /run
/dev/sda1    3778616     1628296   1938660     46%   /
tmpfs        1026268     0         1026268     0%    /dev/s
tmpfs        5120        0         5120        0%    /run/lo
tmpfs        1026268     0         1026268     0%    /sys/fs
/dev/sda5    463826      2316      433043      1%    /tmp
/dev/sda7    15035192    327488    13924244    3%    /home
/dev/sda6    9545920     461072    8580224     6%    /var
tmpfs        205252      0         205252      0%    /run/us
```

Similarly, **du** (disk usage) calculates the amount of disk space that is used by a directory. The regular output states the value for every single entry and can be a bit confusing. To get a summary for a directory, extend the command line call by the three parameters -s (summary), -c (total), and -h (human-readable).

Mounting a Filesystem

Before a filesystem can be used, it must be mounted as part of the directory tree. Most of the time, this is done automatically at startup but can also be done manually. We briefly looked at the commands used for manual mounting at the end of the previous chapter, but we will go into more detail on their usage here. To demonstrate, we will mount the first partition of the second SCSI disk (/deb/sdb1) as /space. Firstly, in order to mount a filesystem you must be in root. Next, if the directory /space does not exist yet, we must create it using **mkdir** as follows:

```
# mkdir /space
```

Then run the **mount** command to include this directory:

```
# mount /dev/sdb1 /space
```

Most of the time Linux detects the filesystem type automatically. If this is not the case and the type is not detected automatically, use the -t parameter (short for --type) followed by the name of the filesystem type to force it. This step assumes that the relevant filesystem type is installed and recognized by the Linux kernel. To list all the filesystems supported by the Linux kernel, the combination of the commands **cat**, **awk**, **sed**, **ls**, and **sort** can be used as shown below.

Of the commands not discussed yet, **sort** is used to sort files in a specified order and will be discussed in more detail in Chapter 7. We will not be going into much detail on **awk** and **sed** other than this example, as this is outside the scope of this guide. In this example, they are essentially used to clean up the data to be more usable.

```
$ (cat /proc/filesystems | awk '{print $NF}' | sed '/^$/d';
ls -1 /lib/modules/$(uname -r)/ -kernel/fs) | sort -u
9p
adfs
affs
afs
```

```
aufs
autofs
autofs4
bdev
befs
bfs
binfmt_misc
binfmt_misc.ko
btrfs
cachefiles
...
$
```

The following command extends the previous commands in order to mount the first partition of the second SCSI disk (/deb/ sdb1) as /space using an ext3 filesystem:

```
# mount -t ext3 /dev/sdb1 /space
```

Unmounting a Filesystem

If the filesystem is busy or in use, it cannot be unmounted. To find out which programs are using the filesystem the **lsof** command from the *lsof* package comes into play. *lsof* is short for *list of open files*. The example below demonstrates how to use the command, and shows this for the directory /home/user/Music.

```
$ lsof /home/user/Music/
COMM  PID   USR   FD   TYPE DEV SIZE NODE  NAME
bash  604   user  cwd  DIR  8,8 4096 260620 /home/
lsof  2611  user  cwd  DIR  8,8 4096 260620 /home/
lsof  2612  user  cwd  DIR  8,8 4096 260620 /home/
$
```

This gives a list of programs that are using the directory. Also, if a user is working in that directory, you will have to change the directory with the **cd** command. To unmount the directory /space which we mounted in the previous section, you must again be logged in as a root user.

Next, test if any other programs are using /space by invoking the command **lsof /space**. If any programs are running, stop them and try again. Also, make sure that no terminals are connected to /space.

```
$ su
Password:
# lsof /space
...
```

Then type **umount /space**. If you do not get an error message, then /space was successfully unmounted. Alternatively, run the **umount** command with the option -**v** (short for --verbose) to see the transaction message. Finally, type **df - k** to see the new partition state.

```
...
# umount /space
# exit
$
```

Automating Mount Points

To automatically mount a mount point during startup of the system, add an entry in the configuration file /etc/fstab. *fstab* abbreviates *file system table*. The example on the following page displays the content of the configuration file.

```
# cat /etc/fstab
# /etc/fstab: static file system information.
#
# Use 'blkid' to print the universally unique identifier for a
# device; this may be used with UUID= as a more robust way
to name
# devices that works even if disks are added and removed.
See
# fstab(5).
#
# <file system><mount point><type><options><dump><pass>
# / was on /dev/sda1 during installation
UUID=dc78e6f6-8a4f-4be0-9192-e4ca37838765
                /       ext4    errors=         0       1
# /home was on /dev/sda7 during installation
UUID=ac2823cc-a7b4-4bf3-808e-e13401e11eaf
                /home ext4      defaults        0       2
# /tmp was on /dev/sda5 during installation
UUID=faef6770-b865-43d2-b1f6-56352413d7c4
                /tmp  ext4      defaults        0       2
# /var was on /dev/sda6 during installation
UUID=d2f4fd43-4f76-414c-9afa-6a53d4cd1d9c
                /var  ext4      defaults        0       2
# swap was on /dev/sda2 during installation
UUID=9ef7106a-c885-4cbe-aaa1-8e2b77ee73cf
                none  swap      sw              0       0
/dev/sr0/media/cdrom0 udf,iso9660 user,noauto  0  0
```

The columns (fields) in the file /etc/fstab are described below. The resulting information in the example above has been spaced to fit.

filesystem   Specifies the UUID (UUID=xxxxx), name (/dev/sdb1), or the label of the filesystem (LABEL=home).

mount point	Defines the directory where the filesystem will be mounted.
type	A comma-separated list of allowed filesystem types.
options	A comma-separated list of options.
dump	Dump information in file with 0 = off and 1 = on.
pass	The order the filesystem is checked, starting with 1. 0 means last.

Keep in mind that the single columns are separated by a tabulator and spaces do not work properly. Tip: To find the UUID for the mount point, look in /dev/disk/by-uuid.

To add a device to mount automatically, extend the file /etc/fstab by simply adding a line. In order to mount the partition /dev/sdb1 as /space with an ext3 filesystem at startup, add this line on older systems:

```
/dev/sdb1 /space ext3 defaults 0 0
```

On contemporary systems that support UUIDs, use the following line. Note to replace the value of *7ca005b2-a7ff-4757-bfdf-81004d4 072ef* with the UUID of your partition:

```
UUID=7ca005b2-a7ff-4757-bfdf-81004d4072ef /space ext3
defaults 0 0
```

Now /dev/sdb1 will always be mounted as /space at startup. You may wonder what the advantage is of using a UUID. By using a UUID the partition is clearly identified, even if the order of the disks changes later on.

To generate a UUID (or to regenerate a new one) use the **uuidgen** command line tool. It offers two options. The first is **-r** (short for --random) which generates a random-based UUID. This method creates a UUID consisting mostly of random bits. This is the default value if not explicitly specified.

```
$ uuidgen -r
4d545248-cf36-4d24-91ab-64a9ed276072
$
```

The second option is **-t** (short for --time) which generates a time-based UUID. This method creates a UUID based on the system clock plus the system's ethernet hardware address if present.

```
$ uuidgen -t
4afa1166-bcf1-11e8-9a0a-68f728ff3d63
$
```

The **uuidgen** command writes the newly generated UUID to *stdout*. You can copy and paste the new UUID directly into /etc/fstab to have a unique identifier for a partition to be referenced.

Setting up New Partitions

The idea behind *fdisk* and its counterparts, *cfdisk* and *gparted,* is to view the partitions on a disk and to add, remove or edit partitions. In this section, we will have a look at *fdisk*, which is a standard package for Debian and is also available on all major Linux distributions. Both *cfdisk* and *gparted* are non-standard packages and may require separate installation. We discuss the installation of additional packages in Chapter 4 and Chapter 14.

In order to use *fdisk,* as a root user type **fdisk** followed by the name of the drive. The next example shows this for the first SCSI disk named /dev/sda.

fdisk /dev/sda

This will open a screen as shown below. At the command line prompt press **p** in order to print the partitions:

```
# fdisk /dev/sda

Welcome to fdisk (util-linux 2.29.2).
Changes will remain in memory only, until you decide to
write them.
Be careful before using the write command.

Command (m for help): p
Disk /dev/sda: 30 GiB, 32212254720 bytes, 62914560 sectors
Units: sectors of 1 * 512 = 512 bytes
Sector size (logical/physical): 512 bytes / 512 bytes
I/O size (minimum/optimal): 512 bytes / 512 bytes
Disklabel type: dos
Disk identifier: 0x2e4f25d8
```

Device	Start	End	Size	Id	Type
/dev/sda1	2048	7813119	3.7G	83	Linux
/dev/sda2	7813120	11718655	1.9G	82	Swap
/dev/sda3	11720702	62912511	24.4G	5	Extended
/dev/sda5	11720704	12695551	476M	83	Linux
/dev/sda6	12697600	32227327	9.3G	83	Linux
/dev/sda7	32229376	62912511	14.6G	83	Linux

To get a list of commands available, type **m**, and the following screen will appear. Use **q** to quit *fdisk.*

Command (m for help): m
Help:

DOS (MBR)
 a toggle a bootable flag
 b edit nested BSD disklabel
 c toggle the dos compatibility flag

Generic
 d delete a partition
 F list free unpartitioned space
 l list known partition types
 n add a new partition
 p print the partition table
 t change a partition type
 v verify the partition table
 I print information about a partition

Misc
 m print this menu
 u change display/entry units
 x extra functionality (experts only)

Script
 I load disk layout from sfdisk script file
 O dump disk layout to sfdisk script file

Save & Exit
 w write table to disk and exit
 q quit without saving changes

Create a new label
 g create a new empty GPT partition table
 G create a new empty SGI (IRIX) partition table
 o create a new empty DOS partition table
 s create a new empty Sun partition table

Creating New Partitions

For the second SCSI disk, start *fdisk* as follows:

```
# fdisk /dev/sdb
```

To create a new partition type **n**. First *fdisk* asks us if we would like to create a primary partition or an extended partition. We select **p** for a primary partition. Then we are asked to choose a partition number. We select *1* for the first partition. Next, it asks for the size. By default, *fdisk* fills the entire disk and uses the entire available space. We select **+4GB** for a 4GB partition. Then we type **p** to print out the result to confirm the partition /dev/sdb1 has been created.

```
Command (m for help): n
Partition type
     p        primary (0 primary, 0 extended, 4 free)
     e        extended (container for logical partitions)
Select (default p): p
Partition number (1-4, default 1): 1
First sector (2048-41943039, default 2048):
Last sector, +sectors or +size{K,M,G,T,P} (2048-41943039,
default
     41943039): +4G

Created a new partition 1 of type 'Linux' and of size 4 GiB.

Command (m for help): p
Disk /dev/sdb: 20 GiB, 21474836480 bytes, 41943040 sectors
Units: sectors of 1 * 512 = 512 bytes
Sector size (logical/physical): 512 bytes / 512 bytes
I/O size (minimum/optimal): 512 bytes / 512 bytes
Disklabel type: dos
Disk identifier: 0x056efeb2
```

Device	Start	End	Size	Id	Type
/dev/sdb1	2048	8390655	4G	83	Linux

Now let us add an extended partition. Again, type **n** to create a new partition. This time from the menu we select **e** for an extended partition and hit enter for the default settings, partition 2, and fill all the remaining space. Then type **p** to print out the result. Here we can see the extended partition /dev/sdb2 has been created.

```
Command (m for help): n
Partition type
    p      primary (1 primary, 0 extended, 3 free)
    e      extended (container for logical partitions)
Select (default p): e
Partition number (2-4, default 2):
First sector (8390656-41943039, default 8390656):
Last sector, +sectors or +size{K,M,G,T,P} (8390656-
41943039, default
    41943039):

Created a new partition 2 of type 'Extended' and of size 16
GiB.

Command (m for help): p
Disk /dev/sdb: 20 GiB, 21474836480 bytes, 41943040 sectors
Units: sectors of 1 * 512 = 512 bytes
Sector size (logical/physical): 512 bytes / 512 bytes
I/O size (minimum/optimal): 512 bytes / 512 bytes
Disklabel type: dos
Disk identifier: 0x056efeb2
```

Device	Start	End	Size	Id	Type
/dev/sdb1	2048	8390655	4G	83	Linux
/dev/sdb2	8390656	41943039	16G	5	Extended

Now let's create a swap space. Again, type **n** to create a new partition. This time there is no more room for a primary partition, so we can only create a logical partition. We use the default *First Sector* and select **+1G** for the *Last Sector* and hit enter for the defaults. Type **p** to see the result and we can see that logical partition /dev/sdb5 has been created. Type **f** to show how much free space is still available on the drive.

Command (m for help): n
All space for primary partitions is in use.
Adding logical partition 5
First sector (8392704-41943039, default 8392704):
Last sector, +sectors or +size{K,M,G,T,P} (8392704-41943039, default
    41943039): +1G

Created a new partition 5 of type 'Linux' and of size 1 GiB.

Command (m for help): p
Disk /dev/sdb: 20 GiB, 21474836480 bytes, 41943040 sectors
Units: sectors of 1 * 512 = 512 bytes
Sector size (logical/physical): 512 bytes / 512 bytes
I/O size (minimum/optimal): 512 bytes / 512 bytes
Disklabel type: dos
Disk identifier: 0x056efeb2

Device	Start	End	Size	Id	Type
/dev/sdb1	2048	8390655	4G	83	Linux
/dev/sdb2	8390656	41943039	16G	5	Extended
/dev/sdb5	8392704	10489855	1G	83	Linux

Command (m for help): F
Unpartitioned space /dev/sdb:
    15 GiB, 16102981632 bytes, 31451136 sectors
Units: sectors of 1 * 512 = 512 bytes

Sector size (logical/physical): 512 bytes / 512 bytes

Start	End	Sectors	Size
10491904	41943039	31451136	15G

Finally, let's create one partition using all the free space. We do the same as with the last partition, except this time we select all the default options. Typing **p** afterward shows us partition /dev/sdb6 has been created.

Command (m for help): n
All space for primary partitions is in use.
Adding logical partition 6
First sector (10491904-41943039, default 10491904):
Last sector, +sectors or +size{K,M,G,T,P} (10491904-41943039,
        default 41943039):

Created a new partition 6 of type 'Linux' and of size 15 GiB.

Command (m for help): p
Disk /dev/sdb: 20 GiB, 21474836480 bytes, 41943040 sectors
Units: sectors of 1 * 512 = 512 bytes
Sector size (logical/physical): 512 bytes / 512 bytes
I/O size (minimum/optimal): 512 bytes / 512 bytes
Disklabel type: dos
Disk identifier: 0x056efeb2

Device	Start	End	Size	Id	Type
/dev/sdb1	2048	8390655	4G	83	Linux
/dev/sdb2	8390656	41943039	16G	5	Extended
/dev/sdb5	8392704	10489855	1G	83	Linux
/dev/sdb6	10491904	41943039	15G	83	Linux

Now let's change the partition /dev/sdb5 to a swap space. To do this, in *fdisk* type **t** to change the partition type. For partition number we select **5**, and then type **l** to list the available types. The type we want is *Linux swap / Solaris*. Type **p** to show that the partition's type has changed.

```
Command (m for help): t
Partition number (1,2,5,6,default 6): 5
Partition type (type L to list all types): L

0 Empty                         1 FAT12
2 XENIX root                    3 XENIX usr
4 FAT16 <32M                    5 Extended
6 FAT16                         7 HPFS/NTFS/exFAT
...
82 Linux swap / So              83 Linux
84 OS/2 hidden or               85 Linux extended
86 NTFS volume set              87 NTFS volume set
...
Partition type (type L to list all types): 82
Changed type of partition 'Linux' to 'Linux swap / Solaris'.

Command (m for help): p
Disk /dev/sdb: 20 GiB, 21474836480 bytes, 41943040 sectors
Units: sectors of 1 * 512 = 512 bytes
Sector size (logical/physical): 512 bytes / 512 bytes
I/O size (minimum/optimal): 512 bytes / 512 bytes
Disklabel type: dos
Disk identifier: 0x056efeb2
```

Device	Start	End	Size	Id	Type
/dev/sdb1	2048	8390655	4G	83	Linux
/dev/sdb2	8390656	41943039	16G	5	Extended
/dev/sdb5	8392704	10489855	1G	82	Swap
/dev/sdb6	10491904	41943039	15G	83	Linux

Up to now, nothing has been written to disk. To do this, we need to save and sync disks by typing **w** to write to disk. Then we can we exit *fdisk* by typing **q** to quit. Type **ls -al /dev/disk /by-id** to see the newly created partitions. As the next step, we will use the newly created partitions to mount filesystems.

```
# ls -al /dev/disk/by-id
total 0
drwxr-xr-x 2 root root 300 Sep 5 12:54 .
drwxr-xr-x 7 root root 140 Sep 5 07:14 ..
lrwxrwxrwx 1 root ... ata-VBOX_CD-ROM_VBO-01f00.../sr0
lrwxrwxrwx 1 root ... ata-VBOX_HARDDISK_VBb9372.../sda
lrwxrwxrwx 1 root ... ata-VBOX_HARDDISK...part1.../sda1
lrwxrwxrwx 1 root ... ata-VBOX_HARDDISK...part2.../sda2
lrwxrwxrwx 1 root ... ata-VBOX_HARDDISK...part3.../sda3
lrwxrwxrwx 1 root ... ata-VBOX_HARDDISK...part5.../sda5
lrwxrwxrwx 1 root ... ata-VBOX_HARDDISK...part6.../sda6
lrwxrwxrwx 1 root ... ata-VBOX_HARDDISK...part7.../sda7
lrwxrwxrwx 1 root ... ata-VBOX_HARDDISK_VBc544.../sdb
lrwxrwxrwx 1 root ... ata-VBOX_HARDDISK...part1.../sdb1
lrwxrwxrwx 1 root ... ata-VBOX_HARDDISK...part2.../sdb2
lrwxrwxrwx 1 root ... ata-VBOX_HARDDISK...part5.../sdb5
lrwxrwxrwx 1 root ... ata-VBOX_HARDDISK...part6.../sdb6
```

Creating New Filesystems

So far we have empty partitions only. These partitions need to be filled with the appropriate filesystems. We will mount the new filesystems as follows:

```
/dev/sdb1 /mnt/root ext2
/dev/sdb5 swap
/dev/sdb6 /mnt/home ext4
```

To do this, first we create the mount points that we need:

```
# mkdir /mnt/root
# mkdir /mnt/home
```

Then to add the filesystems, we issue the following commands:

```
# mkfs /dev/sdb1
mke2fs 1.43.4 (31-Jan-2017)
Creating filesystem with 1048576 4k blocks and 262144
inodes
Filesystem UUID: 8e70eeac-83cb-43f1-a402-a10fdecab950
Superblock backups stored on blocks:
    32768,98304,163840,229376,294912,819200,884736

Allocating group tables: done
Writing inode tables: done
Writing superblocks and filesystem information: done

# mkfs.ext4 /dev/sdb6
mke2fs 1.43.4 (31-Jan-2017)
Creating filesystem with 3931392 4k blocks and 983040
inodes
Filesystem UUID: e7ab67d6-53a6-4c1a-9ee2-5f36d183bef5
Superblock backups stored on blocks:
    32768,98304,163840,229376,294912,819200,884736,160
    5632,2654208

Allocating group tables: done
Writing inode tables: done
Creating journal (16384 blocks): done
Writing superblocks and filesystem accounting: done
```

Next, we have to set up /dev/sdb5 as a swap partition. **mkswap** creates a swap filesystem, and **swapon** activates the partition as swap space.

```
# mkswap /dev/sdb5
Setting up swapspace version 1, size = 1024 MiB (1073737728
bytes)
no label, UUID=a6e9f014-500b-4659-a45f-86d09238d11c
# swapon /dev/sdb5
```

It is a good idea to give each partition its own label. To do this we use **tune2fs** in combination with the option **-L** (volume label). The partition /dev/sdb1 is associated with the directory /root, and the partition /dev/sdb6 is associated with the directory /home.

```
# tune2fs -L root /dev/sdb1
# tune2fs -L home /dev/sdb6
```

Now we can mount the new partitions using the **mount** command. Type **df** to see the result.

```
# mkdir /mnt/root
# mkdir /mnt/home
#
# mount /dev/sdb1 /mnt/root
# mount /dev/sdb6 /mnt/home
#
# df
Filesystem   1K-blocks  Used      Available  Use%  Mounted
udev         1015136    0         1015136    0%    /dev
tmpfs        205256     3008      202248     2%    /run
/dev/sda1    3778616    1628304   1938652    46%   /
tmpfs        1026268    0         1026268    0%    /dev/sh
```

tmpfs	5120	0	5120	0%	/run/loc
tmpfs	1026268	0	1026268	0%	/sys/fs/
/dev/sda5	463826	2316	433043	1%	/tmp
/dev/sda7	15035192	327488	13924244	3%	/home
/dev/sda6	9545920	461356	8579940	6%	/var
tmpfs	205252	0	205252	0%	/run/us
/dev/sdb1	4128448	8184	3910552	1%	/mnt/ro
/dev/sdb6	15413192	40984	14569548	1%	/mnt/ho

As the final step, let us add entries to the configuration file /etc/fstab in order to be able to auto-mount these filesystems at startup. First make a copy of /etc/fstab as /etc/fstab.bak:

cp /etc/fstab /etc/fstab.bak

Then in order to get the block IDs of the new partitions, type **lsblk -f**. The option **-f** (short for --fs) extends the output with additional filesystem information.

```
# lsblk -f
NAME    FSTYPE LABEL UUID                 MOUNTPT
sda
-sda1   ext4   root  dc78e6f6-8a4f-4be0...  /
-sda2   swap         9ef7106a-c885-4cbe...  [SWAP]
-sda3
-sda5   ext4   tmp   faef6770-b865-43d2...  /tmp
-sda6   ext4   var   d2f4fd43-4f76-414c...  /var
-sda7   ext4   home  ac2823cc-a7b4-4bf3...  /home
sdb
-sdb1   ext2   root  8e70eeac-83cb-43f1...  /mnt/root
-sdb2
-sdb5   swap         a6e9f014-500b-4659...  [SWAP]
-sdb6   ext4   home  e7ab67d6-53a6-4c1a...  /mnt/home
```

Now edit the configuration file /etc/fstab and add the last two lines as shown below.

```
# cat fstab
# /etc/fstab: static file system information.
#
# Use 'blkid' to print the universally unique identifier for a
# device; this may be used with UUID= as a more robust way to name
# devices that works even if disks are added and removed. See
# fstab(5).
#
# <file system><mount point><type><options><dump><pass>
# / was on /dev/sda1 during installation
UUID=dc78e6f6-8a4f-4be0-9192-e4ca37838765
                /          ext4    errors=        0     1
# /home was on /dev/sda7 during installation
UUID=ac2823cc-a7b4-4bf3-808e-e13401e11eaf
                /home      ext4    defaults       0     2
# /tmp was on /dev/sda5 during installation
UUID=faef6770-b865-43d2-b1f6-56352413d7c4
                /tmp       ext4    defaults       0     2
# /var was on /dev/sda6 during installation
UUID=d2f4fd43-4f76-414c-9afa-6a53d4cd1d9c
                /var       ext4    defaults       0     2
# swap was on /dev/sda2 during installation
UUID=9ef7106a-c885-4cbe-aaa1-8e2b77ee73cf
                none       swap    sw             0     0
/dev/sr0  /media/cdrom0  udf,iso9660 user,noauto  0  0

UUID=8e70eeac-83cb-43f1-a402-a10fdecab950
                /mnt/root  ext2    default        0     2
UUID=e7ab67d6-53a6-4c1a-9ee2-5f36d183bef5
                /mnt/home  ext4    default        0     2
```

Then restart the system with your new partitions using **reboot**, and invoke **df** in order to see the newly created partitions.

```
$ df
Filesystem    1K-blocks  Used      Available  Use%  Mounted
udev          1015136    0         1015136    0%    /dev
tmpfs         205256     3000      202256     2%    /run
/dev/sda1     3778616    1628304   1938652    46%   /
tmpfs         1026268    0         1026268    0%    /dev/sh
tmpfs         5120       0         5120       0%    /run/loc
tmpfs         1026268    0         1026268    0%    /sys/fs/
/dev/sdb1     4128448    8184      3910552    1%    /mnt/ro
/dev/sda7     15035192   327488    13924244   3%    /home
/dev/sdb6     15413192   40984     14569548   1%    /mnt/ho
/dev/sda5     463826     2316      433043     1%    /tmp
/dev/sda6     9545920    461532    8579764    6%    /var
tmpfs         205252     0         205252     0%    /run/us
```

Learned something new?

If you found any part of this guide helpful so far, or learned something new that you can't wait to try out, I would love to hear about it. The main way for me to connect with you, is through a review on Amazon. So head over there and let me know which topics you liked most, or even which ones you didn't like. Are you using this guide in your studies or job? I would love to hear about it as well.

## CHAPTER THIRTEEN

Working with Links

L inks are not unique to Linux but are a slightly different concept if you come from a Windows-based system. Links are useful when you require a file to be in more than one place at the same time. Such as having a file in your *downloads* folder and in your *music* folder, without having to create a copy which takes up space.

If you keep large archives of the same photos or videos in different locations (which many photographers and videographers tend to do) using links can potentially save you gigabytes of space. There are two types of links in a Linux filesystem: hard links and soft links. We will explain both of them in more detail next.

Hard Links

Hard links allow for greater flexibility when organizing your files. For instance, you could have your music organized per artist in one location and per genre in another location, without having more than one physical copy on your system. A hard link links a filename to the place on the drive where the file is stored (reference to an inode).

It is merely an additional name for an existing file. Each file can have more than one hard link, but it must have at least one. If no links to the file exist, the file is deleted and the space on the drive is freed up for other files. However, the data in the file is still there and can be recovered as long as it is not written over.

Every filename on the system is a hard link. Hard links cannot point to directories, soft links, characters or block devices, pipes or sockets. If more than one hard link points to a file, they must be on the same filesystem. To create a link Linux utilizes two commands: **link** and **ln**. The **link** command is used solely for hard links. It calls the *link()* system function and does not perform error checking when attempting to create the link. In contrast, **ln** has error checking and can create both hard and soft links.

The command below creates three hard links named *link1*, *link2,* and *link3* to the file *test*. The **touch** command is used to update the access date or modification date of a file and works in two ways: if the file already exists, the timestamp for access and modification of the file is set to the current timestamp. In case the file does not exist yet, an empty file will be created that has the current timestamp.

```
$ touch test
$ ln test link1
$ ln test link2
$ ln test link3
$
```

The output of **ls -i** shows two columns: the inode number and the filename (-i is short for -inode). You can see that the inode number is the same for the four files, and link1, link2, link3, and test point to the same inode.

```
$ ls -i test link*
260930 link1
260930 link2
260930 link3
260930 test
$
```

Furthermore, the **stat** command gives more detailed information about this entry.

```
$ touch test
$ ln test link1
$ ln test link2
$ ln test link3
$ stat test
File:    test
Size:    0 Blocks: 0       IO Block: 4096 regular empty file
Device:  808h/2056d      Inode: 260930 Links: 4
Access:  (0644/-rw-r--r--) Uid: (1000/user) Gid: (1000/use
Access:  2020-09-19 16:51:10.033912519 +0200
Modify:  2020-09-19 16:51:10.033912519 +0200
Change:  2020-09-19 16:51:19.245900960 +0200
Birth:   -
$
```

Soft Links

A soft link, also named a *symbolic link*, is a link to another filename in the filesystem. It is much like a shortcut on a Windows-based system. Unlike a hard link, a symbolic link does not contain the data in the target file, it simply points to another entry somewhere in the filesystem. This difference gives symbolic links certain qualities that hard links do not have, such as the ability to link to directories, characters, block devices, or to files on remote computers networked through NFS. To create a soft link in Linux, we will use the same **ln** command but with the -s option. -s is short for --*symbolic*.

```
$ touch test
$ ln -s test softlink1
$ ln -s test softlink2
$ ln -s test soft link3
$
```

Again, the output of **ls -i** shows two columns: the inode number and the filename. You will see that the inode number is different for the four files, and softlink1, softlink2, softlink3, and test point to different inodes.

```
$ ls -i test softlink*
260931 softlink1
260932 softlink2
260933 softlink3
260930 test
$
```

If you invoke the **ls** command with the option -1 (for long format) the output is as shown below. The left-most column starts with an *l* for link, and the right-most column shows the name of the file the soft link points to.

```
$ ls -l softlink*
lrwxrwxrwx 1 user user 4 Sep 15 14:05 softlink1 -> test
lrwxrwxrwx 1 user user 4 Sep 15 14:05 softlink2 -> test
lrwxrwxrwx 1 user user 4 Sep 15 14:05 softlink3 -> test
$
```

Practical Example

In this example, we will look at how to connect two files using hard links, and how to unlink them again. First, we create a file named *file1* using **echo** and redirect the output. **echo** is a built-in shell command and is intended to output text. The command also prints the values of variables.

```
$ echo "This is File One" > file1
$ cat file1
This is File One
$
```

Next, link *file2* to *file1* and output the contents of *file2* to *stdout*.

```
$ link file1 file2
$ cat file2
This is File One
$
```

Now they are both the same file. Let's make a change to *file2* and see what happens.

```
$ echo "This is line Two" >> file2
$ cat file1
This is File One
This is line Two
$
```

As you can see from the example below, *file1* and *file2* are both treated as the same file.

```
$ ls -l
total 0
$ echo "This is File One" > file1
$ cat file1
This is File One
$ link file1 file2
$ ls
file1 file2
$ cat file2
This is File One
$ echo "This is line Two" >> file2
$ cat file2
This is File One
This is line Two
$ cat file1
This is File One
This is line Two
```

Unlinking *file1* deletes the hard link to *file1* but *file2* is still there and the file will not be deleted.

```
$ unlink file1
$ ls
file2
$
```

Unlinking *file2* deletes the hard link and also deletes the file, due to no remaining hard links to the file. The file no longer exists and the space it took up on the hard drive is marked for overwriting.

```
$ unlink file1
$ ls
file2
```

```
$ cat file2
This is File One
This is line Two
$ unlink file2
$ ls
$ ls -al
total 8
drwxr-xr-x  2 jk jk 4096 Sep 18 08:22 .
drwxr-xr-x 23 jk jk 4096 Sep 18 08:15 ..
```

## CHAPTER FOURTEEN

Package Management

In today's world, software can be quite complex. Part of this complexity stems from programs being split into single components made available as single packages, such as binary data, shared libraries, and documentation. This concept of software development is called *modularity* and is generally accepted and in widespread use. Debian, for instance, offers more than 50,000 different packages.

Package management covers all actions needed to handle these software packages including installation, configuration, removal, and updating packages. It also covers resolving package dependencies (packages that depend on each other).

Understanding Package Architecture

To explain the Linux package architecture, we will be using Debian for illustration. The Debian distribution is known for its stability and exceptional packaging system. The descriptions that follow are valid for all Linux distributions that are derived from Debian, such as Ubuntu, Linux Mint, Knoppix, Kali Linux, Grml, and Xandros.

Keep in mind that the names of packages may differ, so too the distribution-specific package mirrors and the names of package classes. The Debian package management ecosystem contains quite a number of different components such as package lists, package sources, package mirrors, different software packages, software to manage the package setup, and the package cache. These components are explained in more detail next.

Package Lists

Debian contains a list of available software packages. This list is referenced in the file /etc/apt/sources, and for specific components and personal additions in the directory /etc/apt/sources.list.d. As an example, the messenger *Skype* uses the file *skype-stable.list*. The lists use a text format with one package source per line:

```
deb http://ftp.de.debian.org/debian/ stretch main contrib no
deb-src http://ftp.de.debian.org/debian/ stretch main contri
```

Each line either refers to a binary package type (deb) or to a source package type (deb-src). The package type is followed by the package source, which refers to a repository that provides the software packages. Next, the line contains the name of the Debian release, which can be specified either as the nickname of the release or the branch.

The nickname originates from a character in the film *Toy Story*. The branch refers to the development stage of the release, and can be oldoldstable (pre-previous release), oldstable (previous release), stable (current release), testing (next release), unstable (future release), or experimental. After the name of the branch, the package classes are named. The entries for security updates of Debian 9 Stretch look as follows:

deb http://security.debian.org/ stretch/updates main contrib
deb-src http://security.debian.org/ stretch/updates main con

In order to refresh the package list from the referenced
package sources, invoke the following command:

```
# apt-get update
Get:1 http://security.debian.org/debian-security
    stretch/updates InRelease [94.3 kB]
Ign:2 http://ftp.us.debian.org/debian stretch InRelease
Get:3 http://ftp.us.debian.org/debian stretch-updates InRe
    lease [91.0 kB]
Get:4 http://security.debian.org/debian-security
    stretch/updates/main Sources [179 kB]
Get:5 http://security.debian.org/debian-security
    stretch/updates/main amd64 Packages [447 kB]
Hit:6 http://ftp.us.debian.org/debian stretch Release
Get:8 http://ftp.us.debian.org/debian stretch-updates/main
    Sources.diff/Index [5,164 B]
Get:9 http://ftp.us.debian.org/debian stretch-updates/main
    amd64 Packages.diff/Index [5,164 B]
Get:10 http://ftp.us.debian.org/debian stretch-updates/main
    Translation-en.diff/Index [3,688 B]
Get:11 http://ftp.us.debian.org/debian stretch-updates/main
    Sources 2018-07-31-2010.17.pdiff [385 B]
Get:12 http://ftp.us.debian.org/debian stretch-updates/main
    amd64 Packages 2018-07-31-2010.17.pdiff [1,388 B]
...
```

Package Sources

The Debian project maintains an official list of package
sources named *package mirrors*. This list is divided into primary
and secondary package mirrors. Primary package mirrors offer
the full spectrum of supported architectures, while secondary

mirrors only offer a subset. For the United States, the official primary package mirror is:

ftp.us.debian.org

You can view the current state of your desired package mirror at the following address:

https://mirror-master.debian.org/status/mirror-status.html

Package Types

Debian divides its packages into three categories, as listed on the adjacent page. Packages that belong to the non-free category include firmware drivers, Skype messenger, and the Flash plugin. Every single entry in the list of source packages specifies their category of software.

Main	Free packages.
Contrib	Free packages that depend on other non-free packages.
Non-free	Non-free packages that do not provide any source code.

Package Management Tools

To maintain the selection of software packages installed on your Linux system, several tools are available:

dpkg	Used to manage single packages.
apt, aptitude, synaptic	Used to manage packages with their dependencies.
tasksel	Used to manage entire software collections (tasks).

The image below depicts the different levels on which the tools operate and how they work together. The two boxes with dotted outlines refer to the shared libraries that handle the package management tasks.

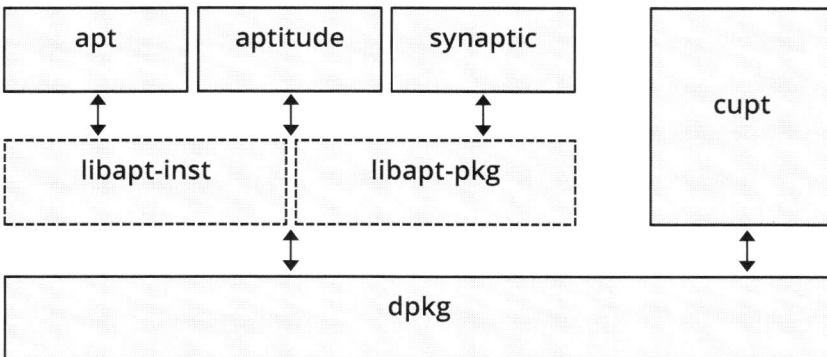

On the lower level, we have *dpkg*. Its task is to install a single Debian package or to remove the contents of a package that has already been installed. To query packages and files, it makes use of the two tools *dpkg-deb* and *dpkg-query*. *dpkg* allows you to maintain your package base but does not handle package dependencies.

Typically, the upper level is represented by the tools *apt*, *aptitude*, and *synaptic*. These tools have the task of simplifying package management by combining all actions into one application. These tools use either the shared libraries *libapt-inst* or *libapt-pkg*, or communicate with *dpkg* directly to perform the package management tasks. This includes handling the package dependencies.

Package Cache

The package cache is located at /var/cache/apt/archives. Whenever you install a software package via *apt-get* or *aptitude* the appropriate package is retrieved and stored locally at this location. To illustrate, below lists the cached *deb* packages using **ls**.

```
$ ls /var/cache/apt/archives/*.deb
/var/cache/apt/archives/cpuid_20140123-2_amd64.deb
/var/cache/apt/archives/libxml2-utils_2.9.1+dfsg1-
5+deb8u7_amd64.deb
/var/cache/apt/archives/python3-bitarray_0.8.1-
1_amd64.deb
/var/cache/apt/archives/python-bitarray_0.8.1-
1_amd64.deb
$
```

The more software you install, the more *deb* packages are cached. It is recommended to clear the package cache from time to time by using either **aptitude** or **apt-cache**.

```
# aptitude clean
```

```
# apt-cache clean
```

Day-to-Day Administration Tasks

This section deals with basic package management actions needed in day-to-day life as a Linux owner and administrator.

Displaying Installed Packages

The command **dpkg -l** lists the installed packages and their status. The image below shows the output.

```
# dpkg -l
Desired=Unknown/Install/Remove/Purge/Hold
| Status=Not/Inst/Conf-files/Unpacked/Half-conf/Half-inst
|/ Err?=(none)/Reinst-required (Status,Err: uppercase=bad)
||/ Name            Version   Arch     Description
+++=================================================
ii  adduser         3.115     all      add and remove users an
ii  anacron         2.3-24    amd64    cron-like program that d
ii  apt             1.4.8     amd64    commandline package m
ii  apt-utils       1.4.8     amd64    package management rel
ii  aptitude        0.8.7-1   amd64    terminal-based package
ii  aptitude-com    0.8.7-1   all      architecture independent
ii  aspell          0.60.7    amd64    GNU Aspell spell-checke
ii  aspell-en       2016.1    all      English dictionary for G
ii  at-spi2-core    2.22.0    amd64    Assistive Technology Ser
ii  avahi-autoipd   0.6.32    amd64    Avahi IPv4LL network a
ii  base-files      9.9+d     amd64    Debian base system misc
ii  base-passwd     3.5.43    amd64    Debian base system mast
ii  bash            4.4-5     amd64    GNU Bourne Again Shell
...
```

The single columns contain the following information:

status	The status of the package, such as fully installed (ii) or removed and still configured (rc).
name	The name of the package.
version	The package version.
architecture	The architecture or platform the package is built for.
description	A short description of the package.

Installing a Package

To install a package, use the **apt-get** command. The output below shows this for the *htop* package.

```
# apt-get install htop
Reading package lists... Done
Building dependency tree
Reading state information... Done
Suggested packages:
    strace
The following NEW packages will be installed:
    htop
0 upgraded, 1 newly installed, 0 to remove and 35 not updated.
Need to get 88.2 kB of archives.
After this operation, 224 kB of additional disk space will be used.
Get:1 http:..ftp.us.debian.org/Debian stratch/main amd64 htop amd64 2.0.2-1 [88.2 kB]
Fetched 88.2 kB in 1s (76.6 kB/s)
Selecting previously unselected package htop.
```

```
(Reading database ... 82741 files and directories currently in-
stalled.)
Preparing to unpack .../htop_2.0.2-1_amd64.deb ...
Unpacking htop (2.0.2-1) ...
Processing triggers for mime-support (3.60) ...
Processing triggers for desktop-file-utils (0.23-1) ...
Processing triggers for man-db (2.7.6.1-2) ...
Setting up htop (2.0.2-1) ...
#
```

Updating an Installed Package

Updating an installed package is quite easy and done in the following way. First, update the package list using **apt-get update** as described earlier in this chapter. Then run **apt-get install** to update the package. If an updated version of the package is available, the new package will be retrieved from the package mirror, the old package will be removed, and the new one will be installed.

Removing an Installed Package

Removing an installed package is done in a similar way as installing or updating. The *apt-get* command has the option to remove the package as shown below.

```
# apt-get remove htop
Reading package lists... Done
Building dependency tree
Reading state information... Done
The following packages will be REMOVED:
    htop
0 upgraded, 0 newly installed, 1 to remove and 35 not updat-
ed.
After this operation, 224 kB of additional disk space will be
freed.
```

Do you want to continue? [Y/n]
(Reading database ... 82751 files and directories currently installed.)
Removing htop (2.0.2-1) ...
Processing triggers for mime-support (3.60) ...
Processing triggers for desktop-file-utils (0.23-1) ...
Processing triggers for man-db (2.7.6.1-2) ...
#

This step removes all of the package content except for the configuration files. To entirely remove the package with its configuration files, add the switch **--purge** as follows:

apt-get remove --purge htop
...
#

Finding Linux Alternatives

You may find that certain programs are not compatible with Linux and were created to only run on Windows or macOS. The great thing about Linux though is that for every Windows or macOS application, there is almost always a Linux alternative. Below are two great resources for finding Linux-specific applications.

https://www.linuxalt.com/

https://linuxappfinder.com/alternatives

## CHAPTER FIFTEEN

Process Management

U nderstanding the execution of a program is essential for being a good system administrator but also useful for general users. In this chapter, we will be looking at processes in greater detail, as well as how to work with and manipulate processes.

A running instance of a program is known as a process. It is made up of the program instruction, data read from files, as well as other programs or inputs from a system user. Every process is assigned a Process ID (PID) which allows the system to keep track of all processes. The system boot process has a PID 0, then the initial process has a PID 1, and so on in a sequential manner. The initial process PID 1 refers to /sbin/initd on older Linux systems or /sbin/systemd on contemporary Linux systems.

Working with Processes

ps and pstree

To list all the running processes, use either the **ps** command or the **pstree** command.

```
# ps
PID        TTY        TIME        CMD
628        pts/0      00:00:00    su
629        pts/0      00:00:00    bash
2507       pts/0      00:00:00    ps
#
```

The output of **ps** as shown above consists of four columns that have the following meanings:

PID   The process ID.

TTY   The terminal from which the command was invoked.

TIME   The time the process has been active.

CMD   The command that was invoked.

The following switches can be used to retrieve additional information regarding the processes:

-e   Shows all processes.

-p   Shows information for the given process id only.

-C   Shows processes that refer to the given command name.

-u   Shows processes that belong to the given username.

```
$ ps -u fritz
PID        TTY        TIME        CMD
1341       ?          00:00:00    systemd
1406       ?          00:00:32    xfwm4
1408       ?          00:01:10    xfce4 panel
1410       ?          00:00:15    xfdesktop
1411       ?          00:00:05    xfsettingsd
$
```

The **pstree** command is similar to the **ps** command but displays the processes as a hierarchical tree. A useful switch is -**p** which adds the process ID to the process name.

```
# pstree
systemd –– agetty
     |– cron
     |– dbus-daemon
     |– dhclient
     |– polkitd –– {gdbus}
     |              |– {gmain}
     |– pulseaudio –– {alsa-sink-Intel}
     |                 |– {alsa-source-Int}
     |– rsyslogd –– {in:imklog}
     |              |– {in:imuxsock}
     |              |– {rs:main Q:Reg}
     |– rtkit-daemon – 2* [{rtkit-daemon}]
     |– sshd
     |– systemd –– (sd-pam)
     |              |– st-spi-bus-laun –– dbus-daemon
     |              |                     |– {dconf worker}
     |              |                     |– {gdbus}
     |              |                     |– {gmain}
     |              |– at-spi2-registr –– {gdbus}
     |              |                     |– {gmain}
     |              |– dbus-daemon
```

pidof

The **pidof** command simply displays the ID of the specified process. The example below returns the PID of the processes that run *bash*.

```
# pidof bash
629 623
```

pgrep

pgrep is the **grep** command (seen earlier) for processes. This command looks through the currently running processes and outputs the process IDs that match the given pattern.

The example below shows two calls. The first call asks **pgrep** to search for the processes that have the string pattern *xterm* in its name and to output the resulting process ID only. The second call uses the two options -l (short for --list-name) and -a (short for --list-full) to show the process ID and the resulting process name.

```
$ pgrep xterm
741
749
$ pgrep -la xterm
741 xterm
749 xterm
$
```

top

The **top** command displays the processes according to their activity. The most active process is on top, followed by the less active ones. The list is updated every second.

The single columns contain the process ID (PID), the user name of the owner of the process (USER), the process priority (PR), the nice level (NI), the virtual memory usage (VIRT), the reserved memory (RES), the shared memory (SHR), both the percentile CPU and memory usage (%CPU and %MEM), the running time of the process (TIME+) as well as the command that was used to invoke the process (COMMAND).

```
                              user@debian95: ~                                    + _ ◻ ×
File   Edit   View   Search   Terminal   Help
top - 20:17:35 up 16:16,  1 user,  load average: 0.00, 0.00, 0.00
Tasks: 102 total,   1 running, 101 sleeping,   0 stopped,   0 zombie
%Cpu(s):  1.0 us,  0.0 sy,  0.0 ni, 99.0 id,  0.0 wa,  0.0 hi,  0.0 si,  0.0 st
KiB Mem :  3159532 total,  2590032 free,   162360 used,   407140 buff/cache
KiB Swap:  3220476 total,  3220476 free,        0 used.  2830844 avail Mem

  PID USER      PR  NI    VIRT    RES    SHR S  %CPU %MEM     TIME+ COMMAND
  400 root      20   0  368348  61944  29728 S   2.7  2.0  65:32.50 Xorg
  511 user      20   0  490724  37948  21540 S   0.7  1.2   0:02.17 xfdesktop
  503 user      20   0  179300  19828  16552 S   0.3  0.6   0:03.64 xfwm4
  563 user      20   0  220316   5760   5168 S   0.3  0.2   0:00.06 at-spi2-registr
  617 user      20   0  631268  37536  27396 S   0.3  1.2   0:06.22 gnome-terminal-
 2576 user      20   0   44788   3588   3056 R   0.3  0.1   0:00.03 top
    1 root      20   0   56912   6752   5316 S   0.0  0.2   0:01.81 systemd
    2 root      20   0       0      0      0 S   0.0  0.0   0:00.00 kthreadd
    3 root      20   0       0      0      0 S   0.0  0.0   0:00.18 ksoftirqd/0
    5 root       0 -20       0      0      0 S   0.0  0.0   0:00.00 kworker/0:0H
    7 root      20   0       0      0      0 S   0.0  0.0   0:00.23 rcu_sched
    8 root      20   0       0      0      0 S   0.0  0.0   0:00.00 rcu_bh
    9 root      rt   0       0      0      0 S   0.0  0.0   0:00.00 migration/0
   10 root       0 -20       0      0      0 S   0.0  0.0   0:00.00 lru-add-drain
   11 root      rt   0       0      0      0 S   0.0  0.0   0:00.21 watchdog/0
```

htop

htop is an additional software package (refer to Chapter 4 and Chapter 14 on installing additional packages) and contains a more interactive version of **top**. The arrangement of the columns is similar to **top**. Use the navigation and function keys to select the processes, sort them, or delete them. The function keys are:

- F1: show help.
- F2: configure htop.
- F3: search within the process list.
- F4: filter the terminal output.
- F5: display the processes as a process tree.
- F6: change the sort order of the processes.
- F7: decrease the nice level of the selected process.
- F8: increase the nice level of the selected process.
- F9: terminate the selected process.
- F10: quit the program.

```
                          user@debian95: ~

File   Edit   View   Search   Terminal   Help

CPU[                          0.0%]   Tasks: 51, 56 thr; 1 running
Mem[||||||||                  176M/3.01G]  Load average: 0.00 0.00 0.00
Swp[                          0K/3.07G]   Uptime: 16:23:52

 PID USER      PRI  NI  VIRT   RES   SHR S CPU% MEM%   TIME+  Command
   1 root       20   0 56912  6752  5316 S  0.0  0.2  0:01.82 /sbin/init
 573 root       20   0  430M  7568  6120 S  0.0  0.2  0:00.08 ─ /usr/lib/udisks2/udisksd
 578 root       20   0  430M  7568  6120 S  0.0  0.2  0:00.00  ├ /usr/lib/udisks2/udis
 577 root       20   0  430M  7568  6120 S  0.0  0.2  0:00.00  ├ /usr/lib/udisks2/udis
 576 root       20   0  430M  7568  6120 S  0.0  0.2  0:00.00  ├ /usr/lib/udisks2/udis
 574 root       20   0  430M  7568  6120 S  0.0  0.2  0:00.00  └ /usr/lib/udisks2/udis
 552 user        9 -11  362M 11312  8444 S  0.0  0.4  0:00.10 ─ /usr/bin/pulseaudio --st
 561 user       -6   0  362M 11312  8444 S  0.0  0.4  0:00.02  ├ /usr/bin/pulseaudio
 560 user       -6   0  362M 11312  8444 S  0.0  0.4  0:00.03  └ /usr/bin/pulseaudio
 514 root       20   0  303M  8504  7324 S  0.0  0.3  0:00.53 ─ /usr/lib/upower/upowerd
 521 root       20   0  303M  8504  7324 S  0.0  0.3  0:00.02  ├ /usr/lib/upower/upowe
 520 root       20   0  303M  8504  7324 S  0.0  0.3  0:00.00  └ /usr/lib/upower/upowe
 507 user       20   0  370M 15160 12856 S  0.0  0.5  0:00.95 ─ xfsettingsd --display :0
 513 user       20   0  370M 15160 12856 S  0.0  0.5  0:00.00  ├ xfsettingsd --display
 512 user       20   0  370M 15160 12856 S  0.0  0.5  0:00.89  └ xfsettingsd --display
F1Help  F2Setup F3SearchF4FilterF5SortedF6CollapF7Nice F8Nice F9Kill F10Quit
```

Foreground and Background Processes

There are two types of processes: foreground and background processes. Foreground processes are initialized and controlled through a terminal session. In other words, there has to be a user connected to the system to start these processes and the process occupies the terminal while it is executing.

In contrast, background processes are not connected to the terminal and do not explicitly require any user input. They hence do not occupy the terminal while waiting to be completed and allow you to run multiple processes. Processes can be initialized in the background with the use of the & symbol.

```
$ process1 &
...
$
```

To send a running process to the background, use the command **bg** followed by the job ID. Alternatively **fg** will send the process to the foreground. You can use the **jobs** command to show the jobs that are currently running and their associated job IDs:

```
$ process1 &
$ process2 &
$ jobs
[1]+ Running process1
[2]- Running process2
$
```

Stopping and Terminating Processes

If a running program becomes unresponsive and causes load, what can we do to stop it and get rid of it? Luckily, we have a few options that allow us to send a specific signal to the program to stop it. The command used in this instance is the **kill** command with a corresponding switch. Among others, we have the following switches:

SIGHUP (1)   Hang up signal. Programs can listen for this signal and act upon it. This signal is sent to processes running in a terminal when you close the terminal.

SIGINT (2)   Interrupt signal. This signal is given to processes to interrupt them. Programs can process this signal and act upon it. You can also issue this signal directly by typing CTRL+C in the terminal window where the program is running.

SIGTERM (15)   Termination signal. This signal is given to processes to terminate them. Again, programs can process this signal and act upon it, for example writing data to a file before terminating. This is the default signal sent by the **kill** command if no signal is specified.

SIGKILL (9) Kill signal. This signal causes the immediate termination of the process by the Linux kernel. Programs cannot listen for this signal.

To terminate and kill a program named *hangingProgram* you will have to identify the program first. You do this by using **pgrep** to find the associated process as follows:

```
$ pgrep hangingProgram
3167
$
```

Next, send the identified process the **SIGTERM** signal:

```
$ kill -SIGTERM 3167
```

As an alternative, you may invoke **kill** as follows:

```
$ kill -15 3167
```

Or you may stop the hanging process by pressing CTRL+Z, and then deleting the process using this command:

```
$ kill -SIGKILL 3167
```

As demonstrated above, this command does the same:

```
$ kill -9 3167
```

Adjusting the Priority of a Process

The processors of your machine can manage more than one task at the same time. We can set guidelines for the CPU to follow when it's looking at the different tasks it has to execute. These guidelines are called *niceness* or *nice values*.

The Linux niceness scale goes from -20 to 19, where a lower number represents a higher priority for a task. If the niceness value is high like 19, the task will be set to the lowest priority and the CPU will process it whenever it gets a chance. The default nice value is zero. You can display the nice level of a process using **ps** as follows:

```
$ ps -o pid,comm,nice -p 1808
PID COMMAND NI
1808 bash 0
$
```

The first column contains the Process ID (PID), the second column contains the command, and the third contains the nice level (NI). As demonstrated in the example above, the *bash* process with the PID 1808 has a nice level of 0. An existing process's nice level can be adjusted using the **renice** command. To reduce the nice level of the process above to 10, issue the command below. Keep in mind that only a root user can apply negative nice values to a process.

```
$ renice 10 -p 1808
```

## CHAPTER SIXTEEN

System and Network Security

The idea behind this chapter is to develop a basic understanding of how to set up and run a secure system. In the following section, we focus on a more practical approach and will have a look at the detection of open ports, existing and active users, limiting remote access, updating software, and making use of the computing power made available.

Open Ports

If you've been following along since the beginning, you might recall that we set up our Linux distribution with a minimalistic installation. We installed only the software packages that we actually needed, and post-installed other software if it was necessary later on. We recommend this for all new installations, as the result is a very lean system with high performance that requires as little resources as possible. The second reason is the limited software restricts the number of potential security issues from inside the system.

As the next step, we will check the number of services that are available from outside the Linux system. This is known as port scanning. The tools that will assist us are the command line tools *netcat* and *nmap* (short for Network Mapper) as well as its graphical version *zenmap*.

netcat

The following **nc** (netcat) command starts scanning the local desktop system (localhost) for available network services on ports between 1 and 1024. The switch **-zv** enables verbose scanning of ports:

```
$ nc -zv localhost 1-1024
localhost [127.0.0.1] 631 (ipp) open
localhost [127.0.0.1] 111 (sunrpc) open
localhost [127.0.0.1] 80 (http) open
localhost [127.0.0.1] 25 (smtp) open
localhost [127.0.0.1] 22 (ssh) open
$
```

nc reports one detected service per line. The results from the example above are the Internet Printing Protocol (IPP) on port 631, Sunrpc services on port 111, Hypertext Transfer Protocol (HTTP) on port 80, Simple Message Transfer Protocol (SMTP) on port 25, and Secure Shell (SSH) on port 22.

Detecting the open ports on our Linux server gives us a slightly different picture. The example below shows the result of our scanning. As you can see **nc** accepts various inputs: a single port, an entire port range, or the service name. If the service is available it returns *open*, otherwise it returns *connection refused*.

```
$ nc -zv localhost 1-1024
localhost [127.0.0.1] 22 (ssh) open
$ nc -zv localhost ssh
localhost [127.0.0.1] 22 (ssh) open
$ nc -zv localhost ftp
```

localhost [127.0.0.1] 21 (ftp) : Connection refused
$ nc -zv localhost http
localhost [127.0.0.1] 80 (http) : Connection refused
$

nmap and zenmap

The next command we will look at is **nmap**. The switch **-T4** sets the timing and **-A** enables the detection of the operating system. This step is called *OS probing*. The following call does this for the local system:

$ nmap -T4 -A localhost

The report is quite detailed and contains information about the detected operating system as well as the services.

$ nmap -T4 -A localhost

Starting Nmap 7.40 (https://nmap.org) at 2018-10-05 10:39
Nmap scan report for localhost (127.0.0.1)
Host is up (0.00013s latency).
Other addresses for localhost (not scanned): ::1
Not shown: 999 closed ports
PORT   STATE   SERVICE   VERSION
22/tcp   open   ssh   OpenSSH 7.4p1 Debian 10+de
| ssh-hostkey:
| 2048 0d:9e:f0:07:f4:86:33:c1:77:24:d6:4b:af:c7:c2:7
| 256 22:83:b2:bc:b2:7d:64:6b:86:b2:6b:e6:c2:d4:45:
Service Info: OS: Linux; CPE: cpe:/o:linux:linux_kernel

Service detection performed. Please report any incorrect results at https://nmap.org/submit/.
Nmap done: 1 IP address (1 host up) scanned in 0.55 seconds

Below we used *zenmap* to scan our Linux system, which provides us with the same result as the previous example. Both results show that the only service enabled and accessible from outside, is OpenSSH (short for Open Secure Shell).

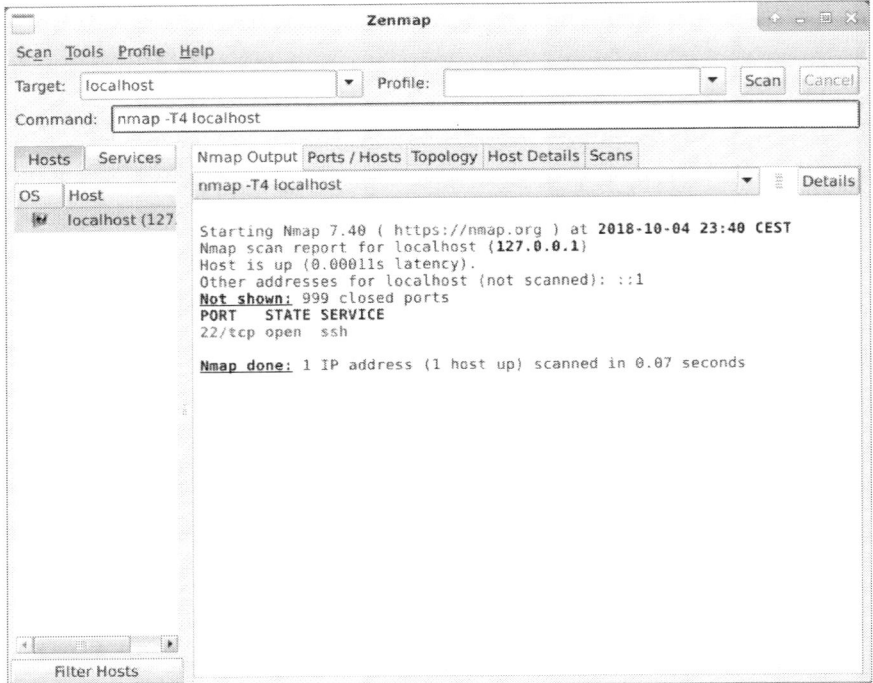

Local and Remote Users

The security of a Linux system includes the users and their accounts. In Chapter 10 we had a look at basic commands such as **w**, **who**, and **users**. Now we will address more sophisticated methods of detecting user information. To see which local accounts exist, you can have a look at the file /etc/passwd and verify the entries. The user ID of a regular user account starts at 1000.

In order to see which local users logged into the system, the **lslogins** command can be used. **lslogins** extracts the user information from the different configuration files and displays the results in a very nice way. Invoked as a regular user without further switches, it displays the user ID, the account name, the number of logins, and the content of the GECOS field. The headings below have been abbreviated to fit.

```
$ lslogins
UID  USER       PROC  LOCK  DENY  LAST  GECOS
0    root       66                      root
1    daemon     0                       daemon
2    bin        0                       bin
3    sys        0                       sys
4    sync       0                       sync
5    games      0                       games
6    man        0                       man
7    lp         0                       lp
8    mail       0                       mail
9    news       0                       news
10   uucp       0                       uucp
13   proxy      0                       proxy
33   www-data   0                       www-data
34   backup     0                       backup
38   list       0                       Mailing List M
39   irc        0                       ircd
41   gnats      0                       Gnats Bug-Rep
...
```

Invoked as an administrative user, **lslogins** adds the information for the two columns PWD-LOCK and PWD-DENY. These columns show if the associated account is locked or if login via password was denied.

```
# lslogins
UID  USER       PROC  LOCK  DENY  LAST  GECOS
0    root       69    0     0           root
1    daemon     0     0     1           daemon
2    bin        0     0     1           bin
3    sys        0     0     1           sys
4    sync       0     0     1           sync
5    games      0     0     1           games
6    man        0     0     1           man
7    lp         0     0     1           lp
8    mail       0     0     1           mail
9    news       0     0     1           news
10   uucp       0     0     1           uucp
13   proxy      0     0     1           proxy
33   www-data   0     0     1           www-data
34   backup     0     0     1           backup
38   list       0     0     1           Mailing List M
39   irc        0     0     1           ircd
41   gnats      0     0     1           Gnats Bug-Rep
...
```

In order to see the detailed information for a specific user, **lslogins** utilizes the switches **-u** followed by a username, as well as **-- time iso** to display the time in a readable format.

```
# lslogins -u user --time iso
Username:                    user
UID:                         1000
Gecos field:                 Debian User,123,456,135
Home directory:              /home/user
Shell:                       /bin/bash
No login:                    no
Password is locked:          no
Password not required:       no
Login by password disabled:  no
```

```
Primary group:                      user
GID:                                1000
Supplementary groups:               Bluetooth, cdrom, floppy,
                                    audio, dip, video, plugdev,
                                    netdev
Supplementary group IDs:            111, 24, 25, 29, 30, 44, 46,
                                    108
Hushed:                             no
Password expiration warn interval: 7
Password changed:                   2018-08-20
Maximum change time:                99999
Running processes:                  32

Last logs:
2020-10-05T12:11:19+0200 systemd[438]: Time changed
2020-10-05T12:11:52+0200 systemd[438]: Time changed
2020-10-05T12:12:24+0200 systemd[438]: Time changed
#
```

As explained above, **lslogins** evaluates the local login attempts only. To retrieve login attempts from remote systems, use the **getent** command. It also evaluates databases that support the Name Service Switch library (NSS) which is configured in /etc/nsswitch.conf and covers services such as Lightweight Directory Access Protocol (LDAP) and Network Information Systems (NIS). To get information for user *caro* invoke **getent** as follows:

```
$ getent passwd caro
caro:x:1005:1005:Caro,,,:/home/caro:/bin/bash
$
```

The two commands **last** and **lastlog** can also be used to show which users logged in last. **last** reports a detailed login as shown below. The columns contain the username, the terminal, and the session information.

```
$ last
user    pts/13    :0    Fri Oct 5 09:41 still logged in
user    pts/13    :0    Thu Oct 4 15:12 - 15:24 (00:12)
user    pts/13    :0    Thu Oct 4 14:28 - 14:59 (00:31)
user    pts/11    :0    Thu Oct 4 14:12 still logged in
user    pts/8     :0    Thu Oct 4 14:04 still logged in
user    pts/8     :0    Thu Oct 4 11:34 - 11:49 (00:15)
$
```

The **lastlog** command prints the statistics for which users logged in last. The first example below shows this for all users and the second example for a specific user.

```
# lastlog
Username    Port    From    Latest
root        tty1            Thu Jul 26 20:35:30 +0200
daemon                      **Never logged in**
bin                         **Never logged in**
sys                         **Never logged in**
sync                        **Never logged in**
games                       **Never logged in**
man                         **Never logged in**
lp                          **Never logged in**
mail                        **Never logged in**
news                        **Never logged in**
uucp                        **Never logged in**
proxy                       **Never logged in**
www-data                    **Never logged in**
backup                      **Never logged in**
...
```

```
# lastlog -u root
Username    Port    From        Latest
root        tty1                Thu Jul 26 20:35:30 +0200
#
```

Restricting Remote Access

Linux has the ability to limit remote access to the system. The two files /etc/hosts.allow and /etc/hosts.deny regulate the access from other systems for TCP-based services. The limitation covers single hosts, IP addresses, and entire network segments.

The file /etc/hosts.allow explicitly allows access, and /etc/hosts.deny forbids access. Because access rules in the file /etc/hosts.allow are applied first, they take precedence over rules specified in /etc/hosts.deny. Therefore, if access to a service is allowed in /etc/hosts.allow, a rule denying access to that same service in /etc/hosts.deny is ignored. The first example illustrates how to limit access via SSH for all devices that have a hostname ending in *example.net*:

```
# /etc/hosts.deny
ALL: ALL
# /etc/hosts.allow
sshd : .example.net
```

The second example limits access for devices that have an IP address from the 192.168.30.* subnet:

```
# /etc/hosts.deny
ALL: ALL
# /etc/hosts.allow
ALL : 192.168.30.*
```

The third example shows how to allow access for all devices that have a hostname ending in *example.net* except for the hostname *login.example.net*:

```
# /etc/hosts.deny
ALL: ALL
# /etc/hosts.allow
sshd : .example.net EXCEPT login.example.net
```

Note that TCP wrapped services do not cache the rules from the host access files, so any changes to /etc/hosts.allow or /etc/hosts.deny will take effect immediately without restarting network services.

Unused Software

Apart from ports and accounts, we must also have a look at the software that is installed on the system. As we mentioned earlier, when it comes to software, the less the better. The idea behind this rule is to keep your server lean and mean. Install only those packages that you really need. If there are unwanted packages that provide services that are not in use, remove them. The fewer packages installed, the less chance of un-patched code and security issues.

Software packages that are left-overs can be identified using **deborphan**. The example below shows that **deborphan** discovered two packages, *iceweasel* and *netcat*. The first column displays the package size, followed by the package category (main/oldlibs), the package name, and then the package class (extra).

```
# deborphan -szP
    235 main/oldlibs      iceweasel      extra
    32 main/oldlibs       netcat         extra
```

Packages that are no longer needed can be removed using the command below. This cleans the system from unused libraries and old dependencies that are left over.

```
# apt-get autoremove
```

Removing unused software helps a lot. It's also important to keep the remaining packages up-to-date, which we discussed in Chapter 14.

Useful Network and System Commands

uname

uname abbreviates the term *UNIX name*. The command displays system information such as the exact name and version of the Linux kernel and the hostname of your computer.

The example below shows the call of the **uname** command with the parameter *-a* (short for --all). The output contains the name of the operating system (Linux), the hostname (debian106), the kernel version and its build date (4.9.8-7-amd64 #1 SMP Debian 4.9.110-1 (2018-07-05)) as well as the architecture of the system (x86_64).

```
$ uname -a
Linux debian106 4.9.0-7-amd64 #1 SMP Debian 4.9.110-1
(2018-07-05) x86_64 GNU/Linux
$
```

uptime

This command shows how long the system is running. It displays the current time (07:36:47) followed by the uptime in hours (21:56), the number of logged-in users (1 user), and the average load (load average: 0.47, 0.43, 0.29) for the last 1, 5, and 15 minutes.

```
$ uptime
07:36:47 up 21:56, 1 user, load average: 0.47, 0.43, 0.29
$
```

To see the **uptime** in a better way, use the option **-p** (short for --pretty). The example below displays a more human-readable version of the information. The system is up 22 hours and 3 minutes.

```
$ uptime -p
up 22 hours, 3 minutes
$
```

ip

The **ip** command (along with the two keywords *address show*) displays the current network configuration. The example on the adjacent page shows the loopback interface (lo) and the ethernet interface (enp0s3). The ethernet interface is configured with the IP address 10.0.2.15. The network interfaces are abbreviated as follows:

Lo   The loopback interface. It is used to access local services such as a proxy or web server.

eth0   The first Ethernet interface connected to a network switch or router.

wlan0   The first wireless interface.

ppp0   The first point-to-point interface, used to connect via VPN or dial-up service.

```
$ ip address show
1: lo: <LOOPBACK, UP, LOWER_UP> mtu 65536 qdisc
noqueue state UNKNOWN group default qlen 1
    link/loopback 00: 00: 00: 00: 00: 00 brd 00: 00: 00: 00: 00:
    inet 127.0.0.1/8 scope host lo
        valid_lft forever preferred_lft forever
    inet6 ::1/128 scope host
        valid_lft forever preferred_lft forever
2: enp0s3: <BROADCAST,MULTICAST, UP, LOWER_UP>
mtu 1500 qdisc pfifo_fast state UP group default qlen 1000
    link/ether 08: 00: 27: e3: 5c: 79 brd ff: ff: ff: ff: ff: ff:
    inet 10.0.2.15/24 brd 10.0.2.255 scope global enp0s3
        valid_lft forever preferred_lft forever
    inet6 fe80::a00:27ff:fee3:5c79/64 scope link
        valid_lft forever preferred_lft forever
```

ping

ping sends ICMP network packets to the given IP address or hostname, and displays the turnaround time. The example below demonstrates this for the host *http://www.google.com*.

```
$ ping google.com
PING google.com (127.217.23.142) 56(84) bytes of data.
64 bytes from fra16s18-in-f14.1e100.net (172.217.23.142):
icp_seq=1 ttl=63 time=36.9 ms
64 bytes from fra16s18-in-f14.1e100.net (172.217.23.142):
icp_seq=2 ttl=63 time=37.9 ms
64 bytes from fra16s18-in-f14.1e100.net (172.217.23.142):
icp_seq=3 ttl=63 time=40.1 ms
^C
--- google.com ping statistics ---
3 packets transmitted, 3 received, 0% packet loss, time
2003ms
rtt min/avg/max/mdev = 36.953/38.353/40.193/1.377 ms
```

## CHAPTER SEVENTEEN

Shared Libraries

L inux, like any operating system, contains collections of files used for different purposes such as binary files (compiled program code), runtime interpreted code (written in programs like Perl or Python), configuration files, log files, libraries, and user data.

In the world of programming, a library is an assortment of pre-compiled pieces of code that can be used in other programs. These libraries contain functions, classes, and data structures. They allow the reuse of code that already exists and has already been tested, so the user doesn't need to reinvent the wheel. As a result, libraries significantly simplify the life for programmers. Among the most prominent examples of libraries in Linux are *libc*, the standard C library, and *glibc*, the GNU version of *libc*.

Linux distinguishes between statically and dynamically linked binary programs. Statically linked, means the routines from the library become part of the program. In contrast, dynamically linked means the routines from the library are referenced only and do not become part of the program. Statically linked programs are entirely independent of one another but require more disk space. Dynamically linked programs are smaller but depend on the reference libraries, meaning they load quicker if the referenced library is already in memory. These libraries are called shared libraries or dynamic libraries.

Naming Conventions

It is common to extend the filename of a shared library with *.so* which abbreviates the term *shared object*. Apart from the filename, a shared library also has a library name known as a *soname*. As an example, the soname for *libc* is *libc.so.6*. Here *lib* is the prefix, *c* is a descriptive name, *so* is short for shared object, and *6* is the version of the library (the version of the Application Binary Interface or ABI). The filename including the path is /lib64/libc.so.6. Note that the soname is a symbolic link to the filename. Usually these files reside in the following directories:

default paths	/usr/local/lib
	/usr/local/lib64
	/usr/lib
	/usr/lib64
system startup libraries	/lib
	/lib64

Programmers can however install libraries in custom locations. The library path is defined in the configuration file /etc/ld.so.conf. Defining the library location can be done in the following manner:

```
$ cat /etc/ld.so.conf
include /etc/ld.so.conf.d/*.conf
$
```

The following command illustrates how to find the shared libraries on your Linux system using the **find** command:

```
$ find / -name *.so
/lib/klibc-IpHGKKbZiB_yZ7GPagmQz2GwVAQ.so
/lib/security/pam_vbox.so
/lib/security/pam_gnome_keyring.so
/lib/x86_64-linux-gnu/libnss_hesiod-2.19.so
/lib/x86_64-linux-gnu/libnss_compat-2.19.so
/lib/x86_64-linux-gnu/libnss_files-2.19.so
/lib/x86_64-linux-gnu/libnss_dns-2.19.so
/lib/x86_64-linux-gnu/security/pam_namespace.so
/lib/x86_64-linux-gnu/security/pam_env.so
/lib/x86_64-linux-gnu/security/pam_filter.so
...
$
```

Identifying Referenced Libraries using ldd

To find out which shared objects a binary file uses, we can use the command **ldd**. For example, to find the shared objects of the file manager Midnight Commander (mc), type **ldd /usr/bin/mc**. Each line within the output consists of the so-name followed by the filename and the hash value in brackets.

```
$ ldd /usr/bin/mc
linux-vdso.so.1 (0x00007ffd555fb000)
libslang.so.2 => /lib/x86_64-linux-gnu/libslang.so.2 (0x000
libgpm.so.2 => /usr/lib/x86_64-linux-gnu/libgpm.so.2 (0x0
libext2fs.so.2 => /lib/x86_64-linux-gnu/libext2fs.so.2 (0x00
libssh2.so.1 => /usr/lib/x86_64-linux-gnu/libssh2.so.1 (0x0
libgmodule-2.0.so.0 => /usr/lib/x86_64-linux-gnu/libgmod
libglib-2.0.so.0 => /lib/x86_64-linux-gnu/libglib-2.0.so.0 (0x
libpthread.so.0 => /lib/x86_64-linux-gnu/libpthread.so.0 (0
libc.so.6 => /lib/x86_64-linux-gnu/libc.so.6 (0x00007f483c
```

```
libdl.so.2 => /lib/x86_64-linux-gnu/libdl.so.2 (0x00007f483
libm.so.6 => /lib/x86_64-linux-gnu/libm.so.6 (0x00007f483
libcom_err.so.2 => /lib/x86_64-linux-gnu/libcom_err.so.2 (
libz.so.1 => /lib/x86_64-linux-gnu/libz.so.1 (0x00007f483b
$
```

If the binary file is a statically linked program, the output of **ldd** is as follows:

```
$ ldd /usr/bin/ldd
not a dynamic executable
$
```

Identifying Referenced Libraries using objdump

An alternative to **ldd** is **objdump**. The following example combines **objdump** and **grep** in order to filter only the lines that contain the required shared objects. The program *mc* requires the eight shared libraries seen below. **grep** will be discussed in greater detail in Chapter 7. For now, know that the command works on text data as a filter and only prints the lines of text that match the specified characters.

```
$ objdump -p /usr/bin/mc | grep NEEDED
NEEDED          libslang.so.2
NEEDED          libgpm.so.2
NEEDED          libext2fs.so.2
NEEDED          libssh2.so.1
NEEDED          libgmodule-2.0.so.0
NEEDED          libglib-2.0.so.0
NEEDED          libpthread.so.0
$
```

## CHAPTER EIGHTEEN

Log Files

There are moments in Linux administration when you will have to figure out why your system behaves in a rather unexpected way. This is where log files come in. These kinds of files record the behavior of the system and help you to find out what happened at any point in time. The log files are stored in the directory /var/log. Which log files are important for you will depend on your system and your requirements.

Important Log Files

The log files explained below are, among others, the most important in server systems.

/var/log/messages

This is the most important log file in Linux. It persistently records generic system events, such as system error messages, system startups and shutdowns, as well as changes in the network configuration. The example that follows contains the log messages that are recorded as soon as a phone (USB device) is connected.

...

Oct 4 15:10:37 debian106 kernel: [532994.056321] usb 2-2:
USB disconnect, device number -16

Oct 4 15:10:37 debian106 kernel: [532994.391279] usb 2-2:
new high-speed USB device -number 17 using xhci_hcd

Oct 4 15:10:37 debian106 kernel: [532994.520991] usb 2-2:
New USB device found, -idVendor=04e8, idProduct=6860

Oct 4 15:10:37 debian106 kernel: [532994.520993] usb 2-2:
New USB device strings: Mfr -=1, Product=2, Serial Num
ber=3

Oct 4 15:10:37 debian106 kernel: [532994.520994] usb 2-2:
Product: SAMSUNG_Android

Oct 4 15:10:37 debian106 kernel: [532994.520995] usb 2-2:
Manufacturer: SAMSUNG

...

/var/log/lastlog

This file records which user logged into the Linux system.
Use the **lastlog** command to see the login statistics. We discussed this command in greater detail in Chapter 16.

/var/log/auth.log

All authentication-related events in Debian and Ubuntu
servers are logged here. If you are looking for anything involv-
ing the user authorization mechanism, you can find it in this log
file.

...

Oct 1 07:30:01 debian106 CRON[4251]: pam_unix(cron: ses
sion): session opened for user root by (uid=0)

Oct 1 07:30:01 debian106 CRON[4251]: pam_unix(cron: ses
sion): session closed for user root

Oct 1 09:04:14 debian106 systemd-logind[323]: Operation
'sleep' finished.

Oct 1 15:09:03 debian106 systemd-logind[342]: Watching
  system buttons on /dev/input/event3 (Power Button)
Oct 1 15:09:03 debian106 systemd-logind[342]: Watching
  system buttons on /dev/input/event4 (Sleep Button)
Oct 1 15:09:03 debian106 systemd-logind[342]: Watching
  system buttons on /dev/input/event5 (Video Bus)
...

/var/log/kern.log

Here you will find messages that relate to the Linux kernel.

...
Oct 8 19:19:34 debian106 kernel: [893330.867019] usb 2-1:
  new low-speed USB device -number 37 using xhci_hcd
Oct 8 19:19:34 debian106 kernel: [893331.000139] usb 2-1:
  New USB device found, -idVendor=046d, idProduct=c03d
Oct 8 19:19:34 debian106 kernel: [893331.000142] usb 2-1:
  New USB device strings: Mfr -=1, Product=2, Serial
  Number=0
Oct 8 19:19:34 debian106 kernel: [893331.000144] usb 2-1:
  Product: USB-PS/2 Optical -Mouse
Oct 8 19:19:34 debian106 kernel: [893331.000145] usb 2-1:
  Manufacturer: Logitech
Oct 8 19:19:34 debian106 kernel: [893331.000259] usb 2-1:
  ep 0x81 - rounding interval -to 64 microframes, ep desc
  says 80 microframes
...

/var/log/dpkg.log

This file belongs to *dpkg* (which we discussed in Chapter 14) and records the changes relating to installed, updated, and removed packages.

...

2020-10-06 21:52:41 startup packages configure

2020-10-06 21:53:21 startup archives unpack

2020-10-06 21:53:21 upgrade php5-gd:amd64 5.6.36+dfsg-0+ deb8u1 5.6.38+dfsg-0+deb8u1

2020-10-06 21:53:21 status triggers-pending libapache2-mod-php5:amd64 5.6.36+dfsg-0+ -deb8u1

2020-10-06 21:53:21 status half-configured php5-gd:amd64 5.6.36+dfsg-0+deb8u1

2020-10-06 21:53:21 status unpacked php5-gd:amd64 5.6.36+ dfsg-0+deb8u1

2020-10-06 21:53:21 status half-installed php5-gd:amd64 5.6.36+dfsg-0+deb8u1

...

/var/log/apt/history

Similar to the previous file, this file records the changes made by *apt* relating to installed, updated, and removed packages.

....

Start-Date: 2018-10-06 21:50:02

Upgrade: imagemagick-6.q16:amd64 (6.8.9.9-5+deb8u13, 6.8.9.9-5+deb8u14), imagemagick: -amd64 (6.8.9.9-5+ deb8u13, 6.8.9.9-5+deb8u14)

End-Date: 2018-10-06 21:50:04

Start-Date: 2018-10-06 21:51:05

Upgrade: bind9-host:amd64 (9.9.5.dfsg-9+deb8u15, 9.9.5.dfsg -9+deb8u16), liblwres90: -amd64 (9.9.5.dfsg-9+deb8u15, 9.9.5.dfsg-9+deb8u16), libdns100:amd64 (9.9.5.dfsg-9+ - deb8u15, 9.9.5.dfsg-9+deb8u16), libisccfg90:amd64

End-Date: 2018-10-06 21:51:07

....

Essential Commands & Graphical Tools

In addition to the log files covered above, there are system commands available to display relevant information for your machine.

dmesg

As covered in Chapter 8, this command allows you to view the entire boot process including BIOS messages.

```
# dmesg
```

journalctl -b

Also covered in Chapter 8, this command shows the boot messages of the system.

```
# journalctl -b
```

journalctl _UID=1000

This command shows the log entries for a specific user. In this instance, it shows the entries for the user with the User ID *1000*.

```
# journalctl _UID=1000
```

journalctl --disk-usage

To see how much disk space is needed to store the log files, use the switch **--disk-usage** as follows:

```
# journalctl --disk-usage
Archived and active journals take up 11.5M in the file system.
```

For system administrators, it is quite common to use command line tools like **tail**, *cat*, or **grep**. But if you prefer graphical tools, two great options to consider are the log file navigators *lnav* or *glogg*, both displayed below.

## CHAPTER NINETEEN

Getting Help

L inux is a rather complex operating system, especially for beginners. When you get started, the list of programs can be quite confusing. Each program has a longer list of parameters or options than the last. And they are not easy to memorize, they have long and short names, and are not standardized. Asking for help when you get stuck is not a mistake or sign of defeat.

To get help on your Linux system, there are several ways to go about it. This includes the manual pages (called man pages), information pages (called info pages), as well as the integrated help of each command. In this chapter we will have a closer look at these help systems and get familiar with the commands **man**, **info**, **whereis**, and **whatis**.

Man Pages

Man pages are the traditional way of distributing documentation about programs. The term *man page* is short for *manual page*, as they correspond to the pages of the printed manual. Man pages are part of the basic installation of your Linux system. The corresponding Debian package is named *manpages*.

A man page corresponds to a specific section in the full UNIX manual: 1 for commands, 2 for system calls, etc. To get information regarding a specific command, open the corresponding man page in a terminal window. As an example, for the **cp** command it is done as follows:

$ man cp

The resulting man page looks like this:

The key bindings are similar to the ones from the text editor *vi(m)*. Use the navigation keys to scroll up and down, and **q** to exit the man page and to return to the terminal.

Info Pages

Info is the default format for documentation inside the GNU project. In the early 1990s, the GNU project decided that the *man page* system was outdated and wrote the **info** command to replace it. **info** has basic hyperlinking features and a simpler markup language to use (compared to the *troff* system used for man pages). Nowadays both systems exist in parallel.

The basic installation of Debian does not contain the info pages. In order to use it, post-install the package named *info* (refer to Chapter 4 and Chapter 14 on how to install additional packages). To get information regarding a specific command, open the corresponding info page in a terminal window. As an example, for the **cp** command it is done as shown below:

```
$ info cp
```

Integrated Help

Aside from **man** and **info**, many commands have an option -h (short for --help). Calling the command with this option opens a specific help section. The example below shows the built-in help of the **uname** command.

```
$ uname --help
Usage: uname [OPTION] ...
Print certain system info. With no OPTION, same as -s.
```

-a,	--all	print all information, in the following order, except omit -p and -i if unknown:
-s,	--kernel-name	print the kernel name
-n,	--nodename	print the network node hostname
-r,	--kernel-release	print the kernel release
-v,	--kernel-version	print the kernel version
-m,	--machine	print the machine hardware name
-p,	--processor	print the processor type (non-portable)
-i,	--hardware-platf	print the hardware platform (non-portable)
-o,	--operating-syst	print the operating system
	--help	display this help and exit
	--version	output version information and exit

```
GNU coreutils online help:
<http://www.gnu.org/software/coreutils/>
Full documentation at:
<http://www.gnu.org/software/coreutils/uname>
or available locally via: info '(coreutils) uname invocation'
$
```

Alternatively, the **whatis** command is helpful to get brief information about Linux commands or functions. It displays a single-line man page description for the command that matches the string passed as a command line argument to the **whatis** command.

whatis searches for the string in its index database, which is maintained by the *mandb* program, and picks a short description from the NAME section of the man page for that command. The example below shows this for the two commands **mv** and **man**.

```
$ whatis mv
mv (1)       - move (rename) files
$ whatis man
man (1)      - an interface to the on-line reference manuals
man (7)      - macros to format man pages
$
```

Another option is the **whereis** command, which is helpful to locate the manual page of the command in the Linux system. It is a very simple utility. The example below shows this for the two commands **mv** and **man**.

```
$ whereis mv
mv:        /bin/mv
           /usr/share/man/man1/mv.1.gz
$whereis man
man:       /usr/bin/man
           /usr/local/man
           /usr/share/man
           /usr/share/man/man1/man.1.gz
           /usr/share/man/man7/man.7.gz
$
```

Every command also provides additional information and configuration examples. This is kept in the directory */usr/share/doc*, and every program has its own subdirectory. The content is standardized and differs from program to program. The content is also accessible for every user. A snippet of the directory is shown below.

```
$ ls /usr/share/doc
adduser                    libncursesw5
adwaita-icon-theme         libneon27-gnutls
anacron                    libnet-dbus-perl
apt                        libnetfilter-conntrack3
aptitude                   libnet-http-perl
aptitude-common            libnet-smtp-ssl-perl
apt-listchanges            libnet-ssleay-perl
apt-utils                  libnettle6
aspell                     libnewt0.52
aspell-en                  libnfnetlink0
at-spi2-core               libnfs8
avahi-autoipd              libnghttp2-14
base-files                 libnl-3-200
base-passwd                libnl-genl-3-200
bash                       libnotify4
bash-completion            libnotify-bin
```

External Help

If the help already provided with the software tools is not enough, and further explanation is necessary, external resources come into play. There are a few online communities that can be consulted such as:

LinuxHint   https://support.linuxhint.com

LinuxHelp   https://www.linuxhelp.com

Another option is *Linux User Groups* (LUG). A LUG is a group of people from the same geographical location sharing their common interest in the Linux operating system. They are organized as a loosely associated number of people or an association that meets regularly. A full list of LUGs worldwide is available from *LugsList* at http://lugslist.com

Linux User Groups

Choose your location

Europe

America

Many LUGs organize meet-ups and events to share ideas, exchange experiences, and to learn from each other. This includes local and international events.

How did we do?

Did we meet your expectations? My wife and I put a lot of effort into this guide, spending many late nights adding examples and tweaking formats, and would love to get your genuine feedback on what you thought about it. Leave us a short review on Amazon and tell us: What were your expectations when you bought this guide? Did we live up to them? What would you change? What other guides would you want to see?

a

ABOUT THE AUTHOR

Nathan Clark is an expert programmer with over 20 years of experience in the software industry.

With a master's degree from MIT, he has worked for some of the leading software companies in the United States and built up extensive knowledge of software design and development.

Nathan and his wife, Sarah, started their own development firm in 2009 to be able to take on more challenging and creative projects. Today they assist high-caliber clients from all over the world.

Nathan enjoys sharing his programming knowledge through his book series, developing innovative software solutions for their clients and watching classic sci-fi movies in his free time.

Printed in Great Britain
by Amazon